THE WORLD'S STRONGEST BOOK

THE WORLD'S STRONGEST BOOK

Ten Rounds
Ten Lessons
One Eddie Hall

EDDIE 'THE BEAST' HALL

ALLEN&UNWIN

Published in hardback in Great Britain in 2022 by Allen & Unwin,
an imprint of Atlantic Books Ltd.

10 9 8 7 6 5 4 3 2 1

A CIP catalogue record for this book is available from the British Library.

Hardback ISBN: 978 1 83895 711 7
Trade paperback ISBN: 978 1 83895 859 6
E-book ISBN: 978 1 83895 712 4

Typeset in Caslon Pro by Avon DataSet Ltd, Alcester, Warwickshire

Printed and bound by CPI Group (UK) Ltd, Croydon, CR0 4YY

Allen & Unwin
An imprint of Atlantic Books Ltd
Ormond House
26–27 Boswell Street
London
WC1N 3JZ

www.allenandunwin.com/uk
www.atlantic-books.co.uk

MIX
Paper from
responsible sources
FSC® C171272

Dedicated to my Nan – Sheila Jackson, my wife – Alex,
and my Mum and Dad – Helen and Stephen.

Contents

Introduction

You know what I get asked all the time? 'Can you lift me over your head for a picture, pretty please?'

Now I appreciate that sounds like a pretty odd request, but when you are known as one of the strongest men in the world, it's to be expected. I usually say yes, too. I'm always very happy to meet the fans and the lift is a little bit of free exercise. Plus, the photos do look very cool. Every now and then though, I'll get asked another question.

'What does it take to be strong?'

How do I respond to that? My entire career has been dedicated to answering that question, and I'm still not sure that I've fully figured it out. That said, I've won multiple Strongman titles and I've broken world records, so I probably know more than the average person in your local gym.

This book is an opportunity for me to go some way towards answering that question, 'What does it take to be strong?' I reckon the best way to answer it is by taking you behind the scenes of my toughest challenge yet.

You're about to go through ten rounds with me – ten lessons I've learned in my career and that I called upon in preparation for 'The Heaviest Boxing Match in History'. That was the name given to the ring showdown between me and Thor Bjornsson, which took place in Dubai on 19 March 2022. I'm going to introduce you to my team, as well as a few of my mates who happen to be elite in their fields. So welcome to the training camp, buddy. Welcome to Team Beast.

I've competed in a lot of competitions in my life, but I think getting in the ring with someone when you're both trying to take each other's head off is a hell of an experience. I mean, I've been in a lot of fights in my life, but obviously you don't set fights up, you know, fights in general life just happen.

Boxing's almost a surreal experience. I found I was

walking into an arena, like the gladiators must have done thousands of years ago, and at the end of the day you're doing it to entertain people. And I suppose that's kind of how I felt, like it was a night of entertainment for everyone. And it was one of the world's historic spectacles, in my opinion. Two of the biggest men on the planet going head to head – World's Strongest Man versus World's Strongest Man. It was an experience I'll never forget.

After the fight, my pal Ross Edgley sent me a message, a quote from Theodore Roosevelt:

> It is not the critic who counts; not the man who points out how the strong man stumbles, or where the doer of deeds could have done them better. The credit belongs to the man who is actually in the arena, whose face is marred by dust and sweat and blood; who strives valiantly; who errs, who comes short again and again, because there is no effort without error and shortcoming; but who does actually strive to do the deeds; who knows great enthusiasms, the great devotions; who spends himself in a worthy cause; who at the best knows

in the end the triumph of high achievement, and who at the worst, if he fails, at least fails while daring greatly, so that his place shall never be with those cold and timid souls who neither know victory nor defeat.

This book is a diary of me daring greatly. It's a record of my two-year odyssey to prepare to fight Thor. It details the highs and the lows, the good, the bad and the ugly. It's raw, it's unvarnished and it's the truth. I'm really taking you behind the scenes and everything that you are about to read is 100 per cent me and 100 per cent authentic.

I'll let you in on a little secret – I had done precisely zero boxing training before I signed on for this fight. You could say I had a mountain in front of me. In this book, I take you with me on my journey from total novice to a professional showdown in the ring. Along the way, I'll tell you about my life growing up in Stoke, I'll share with you what it takes to smash world records and I'll let you in on how much blood, sweat and tears it took for me to win the World's Strongest Man in 2017.

What does it take to be strong? Over the course of this book, you're going to find out. But here's a little spoiler for you. It ain't just pulling weights in the gym, or hitting 12,000 calories a day, or staying hydrated. Sure, you have to do all that stuff. But to reach the top, there's another kind of strength that you have to work on. That is strength of mind. And it can only be developed through time and experience. As I share my story with you, you'll begin to understand how my mindset was formed and the role it has played in getting me to where I am today. Over the course of ten chapters, I talk about harnessing the power of the 'fight or flight' instinct, the role preparation plays in achieving your goals, and how to use setbacks and failures to power you to success. I also take you deep down to the dark place of pain and show you how to break the impulse to quit. I talk about how to deal with complacency, what separates the good from the greatest, and how to seize the opportunity for victory when it presents itself.

I am living, breathing, sweating, swearing proof that it is possible to achieve the impossible. One of my earliest memories, and this is no lie, is watching the World's Strongest Man with my parents and brothers in the room.

I said, loud as anything, 'I'm going to be the World's Strongest Man one day.' What do you think happened? Of course, the whole room erupted in laughter. My older brothers both slapping me on the head saying, 'Oh, shut up, Eddie. How's a kid from Stoke-on-Trent going to become the World's Strongest Man? Impossible. Impossible, Eddie.'

Impossible. That's the worst thing you can say to me. That word gets my back right up. When I hear it, something wakes up inside me. I've always found a way forward no matter the obstacle in front of me. When I hear the 'I' word, it just makes me want to go out and prove people wrong. I don't want to stick it to people in a nasty way, but I do want to show them that it is possible to achieve amazing things in life. It is possible to do things that everyone else says can't be done.

Now, there's a reason some people believe some things are impossible. It's because they've butted up against the boundaries time and again. It requires something special in order to break through what other people see as limits and push beyond them. I should know. It takes dedication. It takes sacrifice. It takes commitment, consistency and self-belief. Those five qualities – dedication, sacrifice, commitment, consistency, belief – they've been the corner-stones to everything I've achieved.

And I wasn't 'supposed' to achieve anything. I left school when I was fourteen. I was a truck mechanic till I was twenty-seven. Absolutely nothing wrong with leaving school at fourteen or being a truck mechanic. School wasn't for me and I learned a lot of life skills fixing up trucks. All that being said, I always had a vision for something more for myself and for my family. I knew in my heart that I could achieve the things I dreamed of. However, any bookie in Stoke would have laughed me out of the shop if I had put a bet on that I would break the world record for a deadlift or win World's Strongest Man.

I got into Strongman around 2007, ironically at the urging of my brothers, the same ones taking the mickey out of me when I was a five-year-old watching the competition on the box. I'd been knocking about the scene for about eight years and knew if I was to close the gap between myself and the freaks like Zydrunas Savickas, Brian Shaw and Hafthor Bjornsson, then I needed to go professional. It was 2015 when a combination of me backing myself and circumstance allowed me to finally do it. It was in turning professional that I felt I finally had an opportunity to land the prize I'd longed for since I was a kid – World's Strongest Man. One thing I figured out very fast was that being a professional was not actually about being paid, although of course it's always nice to earn money from something I love doing. You might at this point ask, 'Eddie, if being paid is not the point of being a professional, then what is?' For me, being professional is about what the money allowed me to do. In my case, it freed me to focus on achieving my goal of winning World's Strongest Man. In turning professional it meant there were no excuses for failure any more. Whatever I did or didn't do, it rested entirely and solely on my shoulders.

At the beginning of 2015, I was exhausted. I was working nearly a hundred hours plus a week in the day job as a mechanic. I was doing something like twenty to twenty-five hours a week running a door security company, making sure that the great and good of Stoke-on-Trent behaved themselves when they were having a night on the tiles. As well as that, I was putting in about twenty-five hours a week in the gym. I was eating everything in sight, every minute of the day, which was partly why I had to work all the hours that God gave me in order to cover my food bill. Not forgetting there was my family – I was trying to be a good husband to my wife Alex and a loving father to my children Layla and Max. AND I'm trying to back up my five-year-old Eddie's bull – win World's Strongest Man. There's a lot of me to go around, but even I recognized at that point that there were too many demands and not enough time. I had a decision to make.

Was I going to be the guy in the pub at sixty or seventy years of age saying – I *could* have been World's Strongest Man? Nah. That seventy-year-old grandpops just sounds like somebody who didn't back himself as a twenty-five-year-old. And I always back myself . . . I wanted to be the kind of guy down the pub who said, 'You know what, I took a risk, I quit my job, and I bet on myself to deliver.' Which is exactly what I did. I backed myself. I bet on myself that I could deliver. And then I did. Sure, it's a lot of pressure, and a lot of risk, but that's the name of the game. It was time to focus on the thing I wanted more than anything else – the World's Strongest

Man trophy on my mantelpiece. It was time to back up my bull.

I sold the security company. I quit my job as a truck mechanic. I had enough in the bank to see me and the family right for a couple of years. The nest egg that I had saved literally bought me the time I needed. I had made serious progress in the eight years since my first novice Strongman event in 2007. I knew I was good but if I were to become the greatest, I knew I still had a serious gap to bridge. For one, I was not as genetically gifted as Brian Shaw or Hafthor. They are 6ft 8–9in, so their frames are primed for adding mass to them. If God was to design two athletes to compete in Strongman events, Brian or Thor would be it. Brian has unbelievable strength. Have you seen him with Atlas Stones? Freak. And then there is Thor. He's a big lad. Enough said. I'm 6ft 3in on my best day. I'm still waiting on that growth spurt I was promised when I was seventeen. Without those extra 6in in height, I had to eat and train my way up to their size in order to even be in the conversation.

For two years, I was obsessed. Winning the World's Strongest Man was the first thing I thought about when

I woke up in the morning, and the last thing before I went to sleep at night. The time in between? Every minute of my day was built towards gaining a competitive edge over my opponents. My mindset was, and still is, if there is something I can do to make even a quarter of a per cent improvement, then I'll do it. It is a philosophy of marginal gains.

These gains came at a price. For one, it meant sacrificing time with my family, with Alex having to take on all of the household responsibilities. Right up front, I have to say without Alex there is no way I could have won World's Strongest Man. She is a saint and a superstar. She took on everything else so that I could purely focus on becoming the best. A special mention has to go to her cooking skills. She prepared all of my meals, no small task when I was trying to get as big as possible by putting an obscene number of calories into my body. I was getting up to a British 31 stone, or if you're French 196 kilos, a ridiculous body weight in any language. It put a massive strain on my body which resulted in more than a few health scares.

Going hand in hand with that was the dedication and commitment to training every day. From 7 a.m. to midnight I was either lifting some serious heavy metal in the gym; or I was eating to fuel my body so it could lift that heavy metal; or I was doing hot and cold therapy between trips to my custom-built hyperbaric chamber to aid my recovery from lifting the same heavy metal. Are you sensing a pattern? My entire life was built around lifting to get bigger and stronger.

There really was no space or time for anything else in my life. Well, that's not entirely true. If there was something which could give me an edge, then I would find the time and the money to do it. You want some examples? I was the only strongman on the circuit to have regular physiotherapy. It cost me a few quid, but it gave me an edge without doubt. I mentioned my hyperbaric chamber which I built myself to aid my recovery. I built it myself because to buy one would cost around £100,000. And going DIY? Just £5,000. Like I said, nothing is impossible if you're willing to find a way forward. I also spoke with sports psychologists who were integral to the development and strengthening of my mindset. When I think of all the things I did, it was the psychology that gave me the most edge over my opponents. I learned that mindset is the one thing that separates the good from the greatest. And my mindset was the thing I had greatest control over to bridge the gap between myself and the best in Strongman.

I was clinical in my consistency and there were some days it was a grind. But you know what? That's part of being a professional. I put myself through an enormous amount physically and mentally day after day. I had days that were a struggle to get through. But I didn't miss one session, training or recovery, in the entire year leading up to 2016. I credit my mindset with being able to get me through it. I was so focused. Well maybe I was just a teensy bit obsessed. Scratch that. I was totally obsessed. I had one job, and I was going to do it as well as I possibly could.

Since going pro, I created an environment for myself where there were no excuses. I put myself under huge pressure to perform and win at the World's Strongest Man 2016. I was very confident going into that competition and I was desperately unfortunate to have a freak bit of bad luck. The day before the competition started, I broke my hand during the familiarization section. I finished third that year. The injury was not an excuse. Other strongmen had won it injured before. But I was not to be one of them.

Still, it burned away in me. I had to be called the World's Strongest Man. I had to go again. I had to win it; I was either going to win World's Strongest Man or I was going to die trying. But I also had to convince Alex. Strongman had taken over both our lives since I turned professional and there is no doubt it was putting a real strain on our marriage. Alex made her voice heard and had very reasonable reservations about my push to come back and win it in 2017. She also knew I was never going to quit. So, we agreed together, it was to be another year of sacrifice, dedication, commitment, consistency and self-belief. Another 365 days in pursuit of this goal.

Five weeks before the 2017 World's Strongest Man, Alex and I weren't speaking to each other. I mean we were, but every conversation was about the competition. Every waking moment was consumed by this obsession of mine. It was my marriage that was paying the price. It was Alex who was paying the price. Looking back, I'd pushed myself and everyone around me to the absolute limit.

Alex moved out and I understood why. The atmosphere was too intense. I was too intense. This is horrible to say, and I'm somewhat ashamed to say it, but at that point if I was given a choice between my marriage or winning World's Strongest Man, it was World's. Every time. I still struggle to reconcile my thinking. Alex is my everything. And yet, so was winning. I know I keep saying it, but I was obsessed, that was my mentality. I said to Alex, let's deal with everything in five weeks' time. Let me go to World's in Botswana and then let's sort everything out once I get back from that. That's what we did. I'm forever grateful to her for that. There are not many women who would allow their husband to put something else before their marriage. But she did and she's an absolute hero for doing it. Because it freed me to focus solely on winning.

Going into World's Strongest Man 2017 there was so much pressure on me to perform. I'd put everything on the line for two long years. All of my time, my energy and my money had gone into getting me here. I'd put my health at serious risk being the size I was. Now my marriage was on the line, too. But I knew if I could win it, it would change the opportunities in my life. I knew if I could win it, I could change the lives of the people I loved. Most of all, if I could win it then I could finally let go of this obsession that started when I was five years old. If I could win it, I would be free.

What happened next? I stepped up. I seized the opportunity that had taken me ten years of graft, I backed up my bull and I won World's Strongest Man 2017. Rather than elation, the overwhelming feeling was one of relief. I had beaten Zydrunas, I had beaten Brian Shaw and I had beaten Hafthor. I was going back to Stoke with the trophy I'd craved since I was five years of age. It was the pinnacle of my career and a massive weight (literally) off my shoulders. I could finally let this obsession go and move on to the next stage of my life.

We were literally just off the podium when a reporter asked me to respond to allegations that I cheated. What cheating did I do? The World's Strongest Git, Thor, claimed that he was the victim of a conspiracy. He said the organizers of World's Strongest Man wanted me to win the title that year and that the referees docked him points in the Viking Press event to ensure that I would win the overall title. It makes me sick to even have to repeat his lies. Take a look in the mirror, pal, and own your performance rather than creating fake news. But of course, the world loves a scandal, even if it's not true, and that became the story.

Thor tainted my victory, a victory that I had worked my guts out for, that I'd risked everything for. He was supposed to be a friend. He blackened my name. He blackened my win.

Look, he's not a big deal for me. I'd done the work, I'd won fair and square and it all just looked pathetic as far as I was concerned.

ROUND 1

Fight or Flight

'Be normal, Eddie.' I've heard that for years. From everyone from my parents to my wife to even my doctors. But I'd ask myself, 'What's so great about being like everyone else?' I never wanted a normal life. Actually, being normal is my biggest fear.

What does normal look like to me? When I close my eyes and visualize it, it's me back in my old house, I'm back working as a truck mechanic, I'm back struggling to put food on the table and pay my bills. When I think back to that time, it scares me. Because I was not living, I was existing. I was on the hamster wheel going round and round and getting no closer to my own goals. At the same time, I was struggling to get by and yet I was working my backside off to make somebody else rich. That period of my life I was a sheep. I was just like everybody else.

It made me depressed because I felt like I couldn't shift my life in the direction I needed it to go in. I had no control; my time was dictated to me rather than the other way around. I was stuck. I couldn't see how to change things.

I went to the World Deadlift Championship, a Giants Live event held in Leeds, in July 2014. The deadlift had always been one of my favourite events, probably because I'm built for it. My legs have always been the most powerful part of my body. I've found that there's something very satisfying about the whole ritual of a deadlift. The lift makes me feel like I'm using my body the way it was designed to be used.

In front of a crowd of 14,000 screaming fans, I pulled a world record deadlift which, at that time, was 462 kilos. I locked out the lift and soaked up the moment. I'd broken a world record and the crowd were letting me know how much they were loving it. The referee, Magnús Ver Magnússon, had instructed me before the attempt that he wanted the bar lowered back down to the floor. In my excitement at locking out the lift and breaking a world record, I let the bar crash back down to the floor and with it went my achievement. Magnús disallowed the lift because I hadn't followed his instructions. I disagreed at the time, and I still do, but what I thought didn't matter. He's the ref and that's that.

I felt so deflated at that point. I was putting everything I had into Strongman because I saw it as a way to change my life. I saw it as a way to not be normal, a way to not be a sheep. But what was the point? I asked myself some hard questions like 'Why am I working 100 plus hours a week?' 'Why am I training twenty plus hours a week?' 'Why am I spending all my money on Strongman?' 'What do I think it's going to do for me?'

That weekend to go and compete in Leeds cost me £500. I didn't make the lift, or rather I wasn't given the lift by Magnús, so I got zero prize money. A big fat zero. It wasn't like I had that £500 just sitting around the house waiting to be spent on a jolly. Plus, I'd already earmarked the prize money to help with my training expenses for the next few months. To my mind, I'd spent £500 of my money to entertain a stadium full of people and I'd made myself look like an idiot in the process. Was this really how I wanted to spend my time, my energy and my money?

I came home from Leeds feeling so deflated. I was irritable with everyone and everything and I knew something needed to change. I felt I had a decision to make, and my decision was to quit Strongman. I'd been plugging away for seven years at that point and I wasn't even close to breaking even, let alone putting away a few quid in the bank. No, there was obviously no money in it. I felt that I was never going to get anywhere with it. If my life was going to change, it wasn't going to be because of Strongman. Besides, I had a wife and two kids to think of. The responsible decision was to concentrate on my door security business, keep working at the day job as a mechanic and quit Strongman. That was 100 per cent the right decision. I'd have more time with the family as I wouldn't be training as much. There would be more money in my pocket as I wasn't putting away 12,000 calories a day. Best of all, I'd no longer be tormented by Strongman. I'd be free of the training sessions and the trips to Leeds to look like an idiot in front of 14,000 people. I'd be pulling in fifty or sixty grand a year. Not bad for a twenty-five-year-old. I would have an ordinary life. I would be normal.

I sat down with Alex to tell her the news of my decision.

'What are you on about?' she said. 'You've just pulled a *world record* deadlift. You've just proved to yourself that you can be the best at something. And now you want to quit?'

It's fair to say that this was *not* the reaction I was expecting. I thought she'd be delighted for me to give up Strongman. But instead, Alex turned around and challenged me with the truth. As I've said already, Alex is a hero and here's a moment that proves it. She said, 'Listen, Ed, you've broken a world record. Yeah, it might not count because of some technical nonsense but nobody could deny that you lifted and locked out a world record deadlift.' I'd pulled 462kg from the floor and made it look like it was half that. My response to that achievement was to quit? *That* was my final decision?

This was my fight or flight moment.

Fight or flight is an instinctive reaction to a threat. It goes back to when we were cavemen. It's amazingly powerful because it's what kept your caveman grandpa from being eaten by a tiger or having his secret stash of bananas robbed by the bloke down the way.

You are here today because of fight or flight. The brain registers a threat, and it primes the body for a reaction. Nowadays stress is the more likely trigger than tigers. And I hope what I'm sharing with you about all that stuff back then is making you realize I was in a pretty stressful situation.

It's such a primal thing, the fight or flight response, that it can often override the more rational part of our brains and allow emotion to cloud our judgement. How many times have you said or done something in the heat of the moment only to later regret it? Alex rightly called me out over my proposed retirement from Strongman. It was a decision I made because I felt like an idiot. I had said I was going to break a world record. I broke it. Then my record was disqualified due to a technicality. I did it in a stadium full of people who had paid money to see me do it. I felt like I'd let them down. I felt like I'd let Alex and the kids down. Most of all, I felt like I'd let myself down. Therefore, I was an idiot. Or at least I thought I was.

All this stress triggered the flight response. My knee-jerk reaction was to run away and be done with the whole world of Strongman forever. When I said fight or flight is pretty powerful, that's what I'm talking about. It triggered an impulse to leg it from something I'd dedicated seven years of my life to. I was ready to give up on everything I'd worked so hard for just as I was on the cusp of all that hard work finally starting to pay off. I was ready to become normal.

Alex's challenge to me was, what if I chose to fight? What if I harnessed that primal, caveman energy into achieving my goal? Could I use that same stress, and the strength of those emotions that told me to quit to do the opposite? Instead of flight, could I fight my way to the very top of the Strongman game?

Well, what do you think?

After winning World's Strongest Man in 2017, I think it's fair to say I was feeling exhausted and exhilarated. I'd fought for my dream and for my obsession, and finally I had conquered it. It was the culmination of a ten-year journey. I had reached the pinnacle in Strongman. The final push from being good to becoming the greatest began with that fight or flight reaction. The primal energy it unleashed was like splitting the atom. I realized if I could find a way to tap into that energy whenever I needed it, then I could use it to power me to bigger and bigger challenges. I figured out how to do that and a whole lot more.

Then I was presented with a new challenge. A huge challenge. A challenge I could really sink my teeth into – fighting in the heaviest boxing match in history. Over the course of this book, I'll share with you all the insights, the techniques and the tools I developed and utilized to win World's Strongest Man, and how they helped me every day as I became the best boxer I could be.

I've learned that there's a very fine line between the good and the greatest. And I truly believe it was my mindset that separated me from the competition. All the failures and setbacks that I came back from, my refusal to take shortcuts in my preparation, the hunger to get better every day – all of these things came from my mindset.

If you follow me online, you'll know one thing about me is that I always back up my bull. In this book, I'm going to illustrate to you exactly how I do it. I'm bringing you into my training camp so you can learn first-hand how I've used all of these tools and techniques to get my mind and body in peak condition for the showdown of a lifetime.

Why did I decide to fight Thor? Well before I get into that, let me tell you about what happened *after* I was crowned winner of World's Strongest Man 2017.

Winning World's Strongest Man was the pinnacle of my strongman career and the emotions in the aftermath were overwhelming. I had staked everything on victory – my marriage, my family's financial security, my own sense of self-worth. The obsession to win World's Strongest Man had been tormenting me mentally for years, so to be finally free of it, to have finally reached the summit of my mountain, it was pure relief. The family were super proud, I had fulfilled a promise to my nan which I'd made on her deathbed. I fulfilled five-year-old Eddie's dreams too. There were very happy tears shed in those moments after the win. Boom. Done. What's next?

I was surprised and disappointed by Thor's reaction to my win. I thought he'd be man enough to accept that he'd been bested on the day by the better competitor. All the negative press that followed Thor's cheating allegation took a bit of shine off the enjoyment of my achievement. I'd worked my guts out for it, but ultimately, who had the trophy in the cabinet? That would be me. No amount of nonsense on the internet was going to take it away. Besides, I had bigger fish to fry than Thor. I had to get home to see Alex.

As soon as I got home and we saw each other, all the tension we'd had in the run-up to World's faded away. We were reunited and back to our old selves together. We finally went on our honeymoon to Mauritius at the end of 2017, just five years after we got married! It was the first time we could both sit back and take stock of how far we had come together.

We returned home to Stoke-on-Trent and the euphoria I felt from winning began to fade. It's well documented in Olympians or other sports people, once they achieve their goal, they can experience a bit of a downer after that huge high. I definitely experienced that and it's a tough thing to take. It almost felt like grief. I suppose in a way it was. It was the death of my obsession with winning World's Strongest Man. I had to make my peace with it, that the quest to win was finally over. Life moves on just as it should. I'd had my moment of glory and with time the euphoria faded. I was left with a deep sense of achievement. I'd reached a level I never thought possible: for one year I was the strongest man in the world. Nobody could ever take that away from me. I had made the impossible, possible.

What was the next challenge in front of me? What was going to get me out of bed in the morning?

I'd always said winning World's Strongest Man was a stepping stone and now I had the time and the money to begin to implement my vision for the next stage of my career – building my TV and social media presence while staying connected to the Strongman world. Things have ticked along nicely, even if I do say so myself. I've had a number of TV shows commissioned, including *Eddie Eats America* and *The Strongest Man in History*. I'm a presenter on Channel 5 in the UK and CBS in America for their coverage of World's Strongest Man. I'm also very proud to say I'm in a business venture and 50/50 partnership with a hero of mine, Arnold Schwarzenegger. We signed a deal and brought the Arnold Classic to the NEC in Birmingham in October 2021 for three sold-out days.

I hired a videographer, Hannah, to help me create content for my YouTube channel and my Instagram account. Regular postings helped build my social media presence, especially on YouTube where I post new videos up to three times a week. In just over a year, we grew my subscribers from pretty much zero to nearly 2 million followers, and it's increasing every day. That kind of growth in one year is almost unheard of. So yeah, I'd been working hard, making some dough and enjoying life.

One question kept nagging me though. Had I made the right decision to retire when I did? If I'm honest, there was a part of me that missed the deep sense of purpose the pursuit of the Strongman title gave me. I was only twenty-nine and at the peak of my powers when I called time on my career. Churning inside me was the desire to test myself again, to really throw myself into another challenge. But what was I going to do? Strongman was finished for me. I couldn't go back to competing in that world. And yet, I still felt there were more mountains out there for me to conquer.

It started as a bit of joke when I said to Don Idrees at Core Sports that he should put together a fight built around me and Thor settling our bad blood. I told him it should be a proper boxing event with a pay per view sold around the world. I never believed that opportunity would come my way not least because I thought Thor wouldn't have the guts to get in the ring with me.

I was pleasantly surprised when the phone call came from Don inviting me to back up my bull. Would I like to do a boxing match with Thor with it sold on pay per view around the world? Yes Don, I would! I gave him a figure, because I'm not going to fight Thor for free, and a week later at the beginning of May 2020, I had a contract in front of me. I had in my hand the chance to right the wrong from all those years ago. More importantly for me, I had a new challenge to contend with. However, before I could sign it and begin my journey, there was one person still in need of persuasion – my dear wife, Alex.

There's a moment in the 2017 documentary *Born Strong* where I float the idea to Alex of participating in a professional boxing match after I retire from strongman competition. You know what Alex's response was? 'You're not boxing. There's no chance, Eddie. You're not boxing or bodybuilding. That's not happening. Okay. Just be normal.' There are those words again – just be normal.

I know you'll struggle to believe it but nobody was offering me cash to be normal or do normal things. However Don Idrees was offering me a few quid to go mano-a-mano with Thor over six rounds. You can imagine that when the offer came in, Alex didn't want me to take the fight. There were tears. There were *a lot* of tears actually. I think she was having her own fight or flight moment with what was on the table, and I understood why. She knows me better than anyone else in the world. She knows what I'm like when I set my mind to doing something. My obsessiveness kicks in and she's lost her husband again for who knows how long. It was a big ask for her. She's the key player in Team Beast. She's behind the scenes doing so much of the prep work. She's the one making sure I'm doing what I need to be doing. She's the one who picks up the slack so that I can do what I need to do – whether that's nutrition or whatever, Alex is the one who keeps the show on the road. Still, the last time we went to that place, it almost ended our marriage. Were we strong enough to take another year of me immersed in extreme preparation and training?

What was being asked of me wasn't just a knockabout in a hall somewhere. It was fighting against Thor, a literal giant, with the event televised on pay per view around the world. The challenges involved were stark and sobering. I would have to get to a professional standard in a sport I had zero experience in. Thousands of hours of training, ringcraft and technique condensed into a very intense time frame. More than that, I had been training my body for the last ten years for Strongman events, which is a bit different to boxing.

Physically and mentally, boxing asks different questions to what Strongman asks. I had to recalibrate and re-engineer my body to go for six rounds under lights in a sport that requires a combination of extreme cardio fitness, dexterity, technique, agility and power. In short, if I was to commit, I would have to commit everything to it. But then, when was the last time I committed 90 per cent, or 95 per cent, or 99 per cent to something? I'll tell you when: never. It's either 100 per cent or it isn't worth my time.

Alex and I are a team and, after the tears had subsided, we sat down properly and discussed it. I understood and appreciated her honesty when she told me she didn't want me to do it. But I felt that it was exactly the opportunity I had been waiting for since winning World's Strongest Man back in 2017. The fact that there was an amount of money on offer that would set us up for life tipped the balance for me.

A reality of the world we live in is that money is the remedy to a lot of problems. Our son Maximus is heavily dyslexic, he has dyspraxia and he has ADHD. He's going to have a tough life out of it, and we feel it's our duty to make sure he's going to be taken care of.

Alex is the only one around me who plays devil's advocate, and she'll say the thing that everyone is thinking but is too scared to put out there. 'What if you die doing it, Eddie?' It was a fair question. Boxing is a lethal sport, and men and women have died competing in it. My motto had been to win World's Strongest Man or die trying. I'd pushed that maxim to the limit. Did dying in the ring scare me? The truthful answer was, no. Obviously, that was not what Alex wanted to hear. We'd reached a stalemate and Alex fell silent.

The reality was that if I accepted the challenge, I would

give everything to it. Alex knows that better than anyone. So, I said to her, 'Yeah, there are risks, but I will work myself to the limit to make sure I'm at my absolute peak when I climb through those ropes.' I wanted to fight, and I needed Alex in my corner. She is everything to me and there was absolutely no way I could do this without her full support. Then came the clincher: 'It's Thor. Don't you want to see me smash him in his face?' Alex smiled, and in that moment, I knew she was on board.

I wanted something to pour my energy into. I wanted a challenge that consumed me in the same way that Strongman did. Ever since my retirement, I had longed for something that would test my own limits. The offer and what it stirred in me reminded me that I need challenges in my life. I needed something that demanded dedication, commitment and sacrifice. I needed to be tested to my limit. Here in front of me was a challenge which ticked all those boxes and more.

In the end, just like staying the course after my shocker in Leeds, the decision became a no-brainer. I'm grateful to Alex for so many things, and I admire how much she'll push me to consider the good and the bad before making a decision. She knew this would be a period of intense training. We agreed together that accepting the offer was the best thing for both of us. Alex is like me when it comes to challenges. Once her mind is made up and she's accepted it, she'll put everything into it. Knowing she was in my corner and giving me her complete support put my mind at ease as I signed the contract that changed our lives.

As a competitor I've been experiencing the surge of adrenaline for years. I knew it gave me extra physical power, as well as supercharging my mindset. It made me feel like there was no way I could be beaten. My focus was so sharp. It put me physically and mentally into a different zone. I could only get into that zone when I was competing and there was always an external trigger.

After the loss of the world record deadlift in Leeds, and the soul-searching that accompanied it, I identified the power unleashed by the fight instinct as something which would give me an edge if I could access it at will. How was I going to do that in the boxing match?

I told you at the start of the chapter my biggest fear was being normal. At this time in my life, my normal was living in my old house, working as a mechanic, struggling to put food on the table and paying the bills. That was where I was at and I needed to change it. The more I thought about where I was in my life and how I needed to change it, the more it ignited the primal energy within me. It made me angry and determined to reshape things for myself and my family. Those thoughts are a way for me to trigger the fight instinct and everything that it unleashes. I don't need a competitive environment or an external trigger to jolt me into action. I can just do it. That's my Eddie Hall patented special sauce.

Back in the day, I was driven by a very deep need to change my life. I knew I had to squeeze every last drop of potential from my being. These days, charged by my experiences, whatever I'm unhappy with becomes fuel for me. I only have to think about where I don't want to be, I only have to remember what it was like when I was struggling, and I feel my heart begin to beat faster and my muscles start to tense, and I'm ready for action. I had a vision for my life, I had a vision for this fight, and I was ready to make it happen.

The fight or flight instinct is a powerful force to try and harness. There were moments when my faith in my vision faltered, and my flight instinct won out. I'd succumb to frustration and the false belief that I didn't have the power to change things. At those times, I'd remind myself that I had no control over what happened in the past, or indeed what was to happen in the future. But I had absolute control over the here and now, and I'd ask myself, 'What am I going to do with it?'

Strongman and boxing are different but even when I was doing Strongman, I was still fighting. I was fighting for a better, more fulfilling life for myself. I was fighting to win. Adding in a bit of that Eddie Hall patented special sauce was what made the difference for me. I used all that I felt was holding me back to fuel my fight to break through.

You've got to have a vision for your life. What's been mine? For a long time, my vision was to become World's Strongest Man. I saw myself standing on the podium holding that trophy, crowned the World's Strongest Man. That became a symbol in my mind, something to galvanize me in my hardest times. It reminded me what I was fighting for. I saw it as a way to change my life and the lives of the people I love, which it did.

Whenever I've set a goal for myself, whatever dream I've had, I've always thought about what it meant to achieve it. I've thought about how it would change my life. I've visualized it. I've seen it happen in my mind. I knew that if I could see it clearly enough in my mind, I could make it happen in real life.

I'm a big advocate of visualization. It is a major tool in my mental locker that I use all the time. I even used it at the start of this chapter. I told you what normal looked like to me. As I visualized, I connected to the emotion of what my old house, my old job, my old struggles meant to me. Those were the circumstances that brought out the fight in me. Sure, my circumstances have changed now. But when I visualize my old life today, it still brings out a fear in me. I never want my life to go back to that time. I never want to be normal. I never want to be that guy in the pub who was nearly this or nearly that. I use that fear to keep me fighting and to keep me fighting forward towards my goals.

This fight with Thor was what I'd been waiting for. Something primal was stirring in me again. I was well aware of the work that was in front of me. I had some time to change my body shape. I'd been walking around at about 180kg give or take since I'd won World's Strongest Man. I needed to shift some of that timber so that I'd have the engine to go six rounds under the bright lights of a boxing ring.

I'd been training and building my body for power events for the last ten years. I never needed any real cardio for lifting, pulling or throwing very heavy things. For the fight I needed to change my fitness in order to keep my muscles and my brain in oxygen for six three-minute rounds, as well as building speed in my fists and my feet. I was at the start of a journey with a sport I'd only ever dabbled in here and there. To reach the level I'd set myself I needed to cram as much technique and ringcraft into my training as possible. That meant learning jabs, feints, proper hand placement and footwork, head and upper body movement, blocking and parrying, inside technique, combination punching and counterpunching. But as I stood at the beginning of my quest all I could think was, 'Bring it on!'

One of the things I've talked about in this chapter is my need to have something epic in my life to work towards.

Accepting the challenge to fight Thor was me answering the call to arms. It was interesting to speak with former English rugby player James Haskell who decided to do an Mixed Martial Arts (MMA) fight after he retired from playing. James said, 'I retired and I was probably looking for something to replace rugby. It was the first time in my life I didn't have a routine. I missed being part of a team and just that general camaraderie. I signed up to do a MMA fight. I basically spent six months training for that first bout and then a month out from it Covid happened. I was super eager to do it from a financial perspective. Now we were looking at empty stadiums for a year at least. It probably made less sense financially for me to continue doing it relative to the other things I was being offered at the time. What I did discover about myself was that I don't mind a tear-up. I was in the cage three days a week doing full on sparring, every day doing jujitsu and wrestling and boxing stuff. So I had a good go at it. My conscience is kind of clear on that front. It's very disappointing that Covid messed up my chance to get into the cage and actually satisfy that itch.'

The great thing about James is how open and honest he

is. He says that it was a bit scary retiring from rugby, something he'd done since he was sixteen years old, but he backed himself to be a success in other things. He knew he had the tools in his locker to take on other challenges. I can identify with what he's talking about. I back myself to succeed at pretty much anything I put my mind to because of the tools I've developed over the course of my Strongman career.

It's interesting, as it always is, to speak with author and adventurer Ross Edgley and get his more philosophical take on why he does ridiculous things like spend 157 days swimming around the UK. Ross told me, 'I have two brothers and I was the middle one. I was always lumped in with my older brother even though he was two years older than me. I'd play football with my brother and his friends and it never dawned on me that I was two years below them. I didn't want to be the runt of the litter. I was just trying to survive. That was my goal.'

One of the things I took away from that conversation was that while you can have talent, you need someone or something to spur you on to want to get better and improve. Ross and I both had our older brothers who made us competitive. I needed an outlet for it, so that's why I became a swimmer, then a strongman and now a boxer. Like both Ross and James, I needed something to channel my competitive energy into.

If you're thinking about taking something on, whatever challenge it might be, what tools have you got in your locker to help you achieve your goal? What's spurring you on to get better? Think about how you can channel your competitive energy into achieving whatever it is you want to do.

Key Learnings

- The fight or flight instinct is a powerful force to try and harness. I want you to think about how you can find your own trigger to fight or flight. What aspects of your life are you unhappy with? Maybe you want to get fitter or lift more. Maybe you want to get into university, start an apprenticeship or chase a dream. I saw Strongman as a pathway for me to change my life. What is your pathway? How are you going to change the things in your life that you're not happy about? Be under no illusion, you are in a fight. You are fighting for a better, more fulfilling life for yourself. It's why you need the primal energy coursing through your veins to get you through the struggle. You need to be able to trigger and access that power every day because that's what's going to make the difference for you. I want you to use those negatives and stresses that are holding you back in your life to fuel your fight to change them.

- Everyone needs a vision for their life. What's yours? For a long time, my vision was to become World's Strongest Man. I saw it as a way to change my life and the lives of the people I love. And it did. It's important for you to reflect on what you want from your life. Whatever goal you have set yourself, whatever dream you hold in your heart, think about what it means for you to achieve it. Think about how it will change your life. Visualize it. See it happening in your mind. I saw myself standing on the podium holding the trophy crowned World's Strongest Man.

It became a symbol in my mind, something to galvanize me in my hardest times. It reminded me what I was fighting for.

- We are all different – we come from different circumstances, we have lived lives with different experiences, and we all face different challenges. It could be pulling half a tonne off the floor or getting yourself out of bed in the morning to face the day. It is *you* who decides what you're going to do and how you're going to do it. I'd put it to you that no matter what you're facing, it boils down to one question – are you going to fight or are you going to walk away?

ROUND 2

Fail to Prepare,
Prepare to Fail

The first person I called after signing the fight contract was none other than my best mate Patrick Gale. We met way back when I was working as a doorman. Pat was a barman in one of the pubs I looked after. We just hit it off and we started working out together. This was long before Strongman was on my radar. Pat's been there from the beginning of my journey, from day one really. Fair play to Pat, as soon as I asked him to be my training partner for the fight with Thor he said yes. There was no hesitation or doubt on his part. He made all kinds of sacrifices in order to help me be best prepared for the fight. He moved into the guest house at Team Beast HQ and was on call twenty-four seven.

Pat is a professional sports coach, my long-suffering training partner and also my best mate. I knew he wouldn't blow smoke up my arse and I knew he wouldn't be afraid to tell me the cold hard truth when I needed to hear it. Obviously for those reasons, I knew I could trust him absolutely. Pat walked the road with me every step of the way and grafted his arse off to push me to get better. He helped me get into the best shape of my life, to face down the challenge of a lifetime.

Pat Gale

I first met Eddie when I was about fourteen and I had just started working at a plucky little wine bar in Stoke called Blakey's. Ed was the doorman at the time. I think he weighed about 18 stone and he looked about 45. One of the first nights I started working with Eddie it was snowing quite heavily. I got a block of ice that had formed on the drain outside, then sneaked up on Eddie, cracked it on his head and ran off. I was thinking I'll be so much faster than this guy because he's 18 stone, so there's no chance he'll catch me. I got about 100ft and then I felt this huge hand grab me. Eddie then kindly proceeded to deposit me in a bin for the glass. That was how Ed and I first became friends. Then when I was eighteen, I started training with him as he was on his pursuit to win World's Strongest Man. We started our journey from there really and I've been by Eddie's side ever since.

I've seen him through thick and thin and he's like an older brother to me. He's always really looked after me, guided me and given me good advice. I like to think that I've helped him as well. World's Strongest Man was a tough ordeal for Eddie as it's such a solitary pursuit. I like to think that I was a good support to him during that period.

Now, I'm Eddie's full-time training partner and full-time coach. I'm with Eddie on every step of his journey, every minute of every day. Eddie himself would say that it makes a difference having someone there to be accountable to, to suffer with through the sessions. Even doing something like the hot and cold treatments, it helps to have someone doing it with you. The cold water pool that we do every night is horrifically cold. It's like sitting in glass. So having someone there by your side to push you every minute of the way just to say, 'Come on, you've got thirty seconds left.' It makes all the difference.

Sparring with Eddie is intense to be honest. It's hard to describe what it's like standing in the corner of a ring and seeing someone of such stature and mass standing opposite you. He's big, he's fast and he's aggressive. When we first started the sparring it was very raw.

One of the first things I did when Pat agreed to train me in May 2020 was get into the ring with him and have a dust-up. Yeah, it was pretty reckless to get in the ring and start fighting, even with the headgear on, when I had done zero boxing training. It's not something I would encourage anyone reading this book to do. But I did it because I needed to know what I was signing up for. I needed to see where my body was at. I needed to know what it felt like to have a big lad like Pat come out of his corner swinging at me. Most of all, I needed to figure out what I didn't know.

I'm glad I did it because straight away I felt an obsession with boxing kick in. I began watching Muhammad Ali fights in detail and felt pumped. Ali was without doubt the greatest of all time and I watched his fights to try and learn from him. How did he move his feet? How did he slip a punch? How did he set his body shape when facing his opponent? I knew then that I had got a ton to learn.

Winning and losing doesn't just happen on the night. It happens on each and every day for months before. Preparation is the key. Fail to prepare properly, prepare to take a proper beating. I had every hour of every day mapped out FOR A YEAR in advance of World's Strongest Man 2017. When I talk about preparation, that's what I'm talking about. That's the standard required to succeed at an elite level. I relished having a new challenge in front of me with the boxing match, and I wanted to get to that elite level. That meant planning. Plans gave me structure, they made me accountable, and they gave me focus. Every morning I rolled out of bed, downed a protein shake with my supplements, and believe me I knew *exactly* what I had to do for the rest day. It was all mapped out.

After that first dust-up, Pat and I sat down and began to sketch out what I needed to do. We came up with three things to work on – my boxing skills, my cardio and my diet. My boxing skills were basically zero; scrapping as a kid on the streets of Stoke didn't count for anything in the boxing ring. I grew up using my fists around town and I was pretty useful as a bouncer. But I knew I definitely needed a solid boxing trainer to teach me how to box properly. Coming from Strongman, which is such a solitary sport, I was used to training on my own and coming up with my own plans for competition. But not this time. I knew the kind of person I needed. Someone steeped in boxing who could get me up to a professional level in a year. I wanted someone who could mentor me, get me up to speed in the sweet science because I was coming in as a blank canvas. I had zero ringcraft and I had to learn fast. I also wanted someone who was going to work just as hard as I would. I knew that finding someone to fit the bill was going to take some time. But time was the one thing I didn't have with so much to learn. So, I started to put out the feelers to those in the know that I was in the market for a proper old school boxing coach.

Cardio fitness and diet went hand in hand. I hired a nutritionist for the first time in my career. Again, coming from the Strongman world, it was always a pretty simple formula. Get as many calories into my body as possible so that I could get as massive as I possibly could. Boxing presented a very different food challenge. My nutritionist helped me plan my diet so that I would have the fuel to get me through training, but not so much that I stayed the same weight. At this point I was walking around at about 180 kilos. I decided that my goal weight for the fight with Thor was going to be around the 160-kilo mark. Meaning I had to drop about 20 kilos.

It might surprise a few of you wet lettuces out there but I'm a sports science nerd and I want to explain to you the science behind my cardio training. There are two types of exercise: aerobic, meaning with air, and anaerobic, meaning without air. Weightlifting and Strongman events are for the most part anaerobic, meaning the strain is on the muscles rather than the cardiovascular system. But boxing is an aerobic sport, meaning it puts a strain on the CV system, that's your heart and lungs.

I had kept in pretty good nick in the years since my retirement from Strongman. However, most of my training had a Strongman accent, if you like; I'd kept lifting heavy weights and I never gave much emphasis to cardio. To get me ready for the fight, I had to walk a line between improving my cardio without compromising my power, all whilst reducing my size.

More science nerd stuff for you – the best way to improve my cardio was to ensure I trained at a level that increased my anaerobic threshold. What is anaerobic threshold? Well, you know that burn you feel in your muscles when you're pushing yourself to the limit? That's lactic acid. Lactic acid starts knocking at the door when muscles aren't getting enough oxygen. I had to raise my tolerance to lactic acid so that I could work at a very high intensity for a very long time before the burn kicked in. The best way to increase my tolerance was through high intensity interval training (HIIT). Battle ropes, kettle ball swings, SkiErg, Wattbike, burpees. All those exercises that really stress the heart and lungs. I wore a heart rate monitor to keep me honest and ensure I worked at the right intensity. My goal was a heart rate around the 160 to 170 beats per minute range as that is the ideal fat-burning zone. One of the additional benefits of HIIT was that it speeded up my metabolism, meaning it really helped to burn off the fat. Combining that with the diet meant getting shredded.

This is the training plan Pat and I put into practice:

VARIABLE DAYS	MONDAY LEGS	TUESDAY CHEST
Rotation 1	Step ups 3 x 8	Flat bench 2 x 10
	Good mornings 2 x 8	Incline dumb-bells 2 x 8 single arm
	SSB (Safety squat bar) 1 x 6 @ 230kg	Cable flies 3 x 10
	Hip thrust 2 x 10 @ 220kg	Sub scrap rotations 2 x 10
	Yoke 2 x 20 metre runs @ 240–300kg	Tricep extentions 3 x 15 @ 80kg
	Ab roll outs x 3	
Rotation 2	Step ups 3 x 8	Flat dumb-bells 2 x 10 single arm
	BSS (Bulgarian split squat) 2 x 6 up to 100kg	Incline bench 1 x 8 single arm
	Squats 1 x 6 € 200kg+	Machine flies 2 x 10
	Hypers 3 x 15	Sub scap rotations 2 x 10
	Ab punches x 3	Tricep extensions 3 x 15 @ 80kg
Rotation 3	Step ups 3 x 10	
	Lunges 2 x 8	
	Front squat 2 x 8	
	Box jumps x 3	

FIXED DAYS: WEDNESDAY: 32 minute HIIT (3 mins on, 1 off), battle ropes, sled pulls, sprints, sledgehammer, assault bike, medicine ball slams, burpees, clean and press
SATURDAY: Boxing only
SUNDAY: Swimming 6 lengths in 3 minutes, 1 minute rest x 6

THURSDAY BACK	FRIDAY SHOULDERS
Deadlifts 1 x 4–6 @ 220kg+	Dumb-bell press single arm 1 x 8 @ 72.5kg
Lat pull down 2 x 10 full stack	Cable side / front raises 2 x 10
Pull overs dumb-bell 3 x 6	Rear delt raises 3 x 10
Row machine 1 x 6	Iron neck rotations x 10
Bent over row 2 x 8	
Ab punches x 3 Bicep hammer curls x 2	
Stiff leg deadlift 2 x 10	Barbell press seated 2 x 6–8
Pull overs cable 3 x 8	Lane mine press with bands 3 x 6
Pull ups 2 sets as many as possible	Dumb-bell side raises 2 x 15
Db row 2 x 8 @ 72.5kg	Rear delt machine 3 x 10
Ab punches x 3	Iron neck rotations x 10
Bicep curls x 2	

For the actual fight preparation, from around 15 weeks out, we switched to full body workouts just twice a week which looked like this:

	ROTATION 1	ROTATION 2
E1	Plank get ups with drops timed by Pat 3 x 6–10	Burpees 15 x 2 Ball slams 10 x 2 Superman planks 10 x 2
E2a	Ball slams – hard as possible with as much time as possible 2 x 10	Hex bar deadlift 220kg x 5
E2b	Ball slams in a full lunge position 1 x 10	—
E2c	Banded rotations 2 x 10 each side	—
E3	Lat pull down 1 x working set Full stack 10 reps	Seated shoulder press dumb-bell single arm 62.5kg x 10
E4	Incline dumb-bell press 62.5kg x 6 each arm	Bulgarian split squat – SSB @ 35kg 12.5kg–20kg x 6
E5	Land mine press 2 x 6 @ 40kg + bands	Incline dumb-bell press single arm 62.5kg x 8 x 2
E6	Bulgarian split squat – SSB @ 35kg: 20kg max a side x 6 each leg	Incline cable row Full stack x 10
E7	Iron neck 5 rotations each way Full weight stack @ 80kg	Tricep push downs 10 x 2 Bicep curl 10 x 2

Here is my diet, which I worked on with Pat and my nutritionist Nathan Payton (see pages 58–9):

The plan was coming together, with lots of pukey cardio sessions to complement my boxing training. The one thing I had in my back pocket, and it gave me some confidence, was the thousands of hours I'd spent swimming as a kid. I was once collared as a potential Olympian when I was a fifteen-year-old and I knew I could do the cardio when it counted. My cardiovascular system just needed a kick in the arse to reawaken it.

Not everything I did for Strongman was completely redundant. I've always been religious about recovery – hot and cold therapies as well as time in the hyperbaric chamber. We decided to incorporate these sessions into my boxing regime. I learned from Strongman how important physio is for my body and my performance, so we threw plenty of that in too.

Getting right down to brass tacks, this is all that preparation actually is: You set a goal and you break down that goal into lots of smaller goals. Here was my goal – knock Thor out. Here were all the smaller goals – boxing skills, fitness, diet and recovery. I broke those four down further into their own even smaller goals.

The way I saw it, every session in the plan, every little

	MONDAY	**TUESDAY**	**WEDNESDAY**	
Meal 1 Protein	275g Smoked Salmon	275g Venison	275g Smoked Salmon	
Meal 1 Carb	4 Slices Sourdough	150g Rice Crispies	4 Slices Sourdough	
Meal 1 Veg	Sweet Bite Peppers	Fried Mushrooms	Sweet Bite Peppers	
Snack 1	3 Scoop Protein Shake + 1 Banana	3 Scoop Protein Shake + 1 Banana	3 Scoop Protein Shake + 1 Banana	
Meal 2 Protein	275g Beef Mince	275g Beef Mince	275g Minced Venison	
Meal 2 Carb	275g Basmati Rice	275g Basmati Rice	275g Basmati Rice	
Meal 2 Veg	Asparagus	Broccoli	Asparagus	
Meal 2 Fruit	200g Blueberries	30 Strawberries	1 Apple	
Snack 2	3 Scoop Shake + 1x Oat Bar + 2tbsp Honey	3 Scoop Shake + 1x Oat Bar + 2tbsp Honey	3 Scoop Shake + 1x Oat Bar + 2tbsp Honey	
Meal 3 Carb	350g Potato	275g Basmati Rice	275g Basmati Rice	
Meal 3 Veg	Carrots	Asparagus	Mixed Veg	
Snack 3	400g Greek Yoghurt (NOT fat free)	400g Greek Yoghurt (NOT fat free)	400g Greek Yoghurt (NOT fat free)	

(1 VEG) UNLIMITED QUALITY • protein weights are AFTER cooking • 275g rice is cooked measure • all seasoning and sauces allowed except white sauces and gravy • green peppers, jalapeno peppers, onions, mushrooms, cucumbers, tomatoes are all free foods – they count for nothing.

THURSDAY	FRIDAY	SATURDAY	SUNDAY
275g Venison	275g Smoked Salmon	8 Whole Eggs	275g Smoked Salmon
150g Rice Crispice	4 Slices Sourdough	150g Rice Crispies	4 Slices Sourdough
Fried Mushrooms	Sweet Bite Peppers	Sweet Bite Peppers	Sweet Bite Peppers
3 Scoop Protein Shake + 1 Banana	3 Scoop Protein Shake + 1 Banana	3 Scoop Protein Shake + 1 Banana	3 Scoop Protein Shake + 1 Banana
275g Beef Mince	275g Minced Ribeye Steak	275g Minced Venison	275g Basmati Rice
275g Basmati Rice	275g Basmati Rice	275g Basmati Rice	275g Basmati Rice
Asparagus	Broccoli	Mixed Veg	Mixed Veg
1 Orange	1 Apple	1 Orange	1 Apple
3 Scoop Shake + 1x Oat Bar + 2tbsp Honey	3 Scoop Shake + 1x Oat Bar + 2tbsp Honey	3 Scoop Shake + 1x Oat Bar + 2tbsp Honey	3 Scoop Shake + 1x Oat Bar + 2tbsp Honey
275g Basmati Rice	350g Potato	275g Basmati Rice	350g Potato
Asparagus	Broccoli	Spinach	Carrots
400g Greek Yoghurt (NOT fat free)	400g Greek Yoghurt (NOT fat free)	400g Greek Yoghurt (NOT fat free)	400g Greek Yoghurt (NOT fat free)

goal, was a brick. And as I put brick on top of bricks, I built a whole house made of gains. Each element gave me a slight gain, each brick made the wall higher and sturdier, but in itself it was not that significant. It was only when I put all my gains together, all my bricks, that I had this sturdy house. By doing it this way, it made all of the hard work I put in pay off in the most efficient way possible.

The other thing I liked about putting a plan like this together was that it made me accountable every minute of every day. There were no grey areas about what I should or shouldn't be doing, no easy outs of a session that I could have sacked off. If it said ten reps, I did ten reps. Not seven or eight. I did ten. Make no mistake, accountability was crucial to my success. When you've got a plan and you've told yourself you're going to stick to it, it makes it really hard to skip a training or a recovery session.

Take my physio sessions which I did every week. They cost me a nice chunk of change. I paid for them in advance so that if I skipped one then I would have lost the money. That held me accountable. My physio sessions were awful, like a form of torture. Do you know what scraping is? My physio had this thing that looked like a knuckleduster with a sharp edge. She scraped the muscles down my thighs, my biceps and my shoulders, to break up the scar tissue. It was an hour every Saturday and it was agony. But it was another brick that built my house of gains.

I was glad I had all that experience from prepping for Strongman to get me ready for the fight. Of course, there was quite a difference between Strongman and boxing, but the thinking behind the preparation was the same. The biggest lessons I took from the preparation that led me to winning World's Strongest Man was to apply myself to my goals, work my guts out and hold myself accountable. With my plan, I created an environment where excuses didn't even exist. I stuck to my diet plan. I never sacked off a Saturday morning scraping session with my physio. Zero excuses. Full accountability. That was the environment I created when I prepared to fight Thor.

There's a reason I called this chapter 'Fail to Prepare, Prepare to Fail'. I want to hammer home how critical preparation is. I always say, if you want to chop down a tree, the best place to start is by sharpening your axe. And that's what I do. I think about every angle and aspect of the challenge I'm taking on. I map the journey ahead and

I formulate a strategy which gives me the best chance of succeeding. Once I have a plan, I commit it to paper. That way, I know exactly what I'm doing at every step along the way. Writing it down makes me accountable to my plan. I always create an environment for myself of no excuses and full accountability. I know what I should be doing at every step on my journey and it's my responsibility to do it. This is my house of gains that I'm building, and I have to own every brick.

The best part about taking that approach to preparation is that it makes things really simple. As I came up with my plan for my fight against Thor, I felt the excitement building within me. The excitement is important as it's a gut feeling that tells me I'm doing exactly what I should be doing. Who wouldn't want to take part in a pay-per-view boxing match in a stadium with thousands of screaming fans? It was awesome!

Whatever challenge I'm preparing to attempt, if it doesn't get my heart beating and the juices flowing, I think again. I need to be obsessed with whatever I'm taking on because I'm living with it every hour of every day of every week. That's how it was with this fight. I was stepping into the gym every time with a plan, and a purpose, and I was loving it. My heart was 100 per cent invested in what I was trying to achieve. It was heart that carried me through the hard days when I was struggling to get through a session. It was heart that got me through the agonizing physio sessions. It was heart that saw me through the setbacks and failures on the road to the big fight. I loved every minute of it.

Team Beast and I created a training plan to ensure my body was in peak condition for fight night. But we also considered the mental side – what was going to keep me and the people around me happy as I put in all those hours of training.

When I was making the plan, I was very aware of how the intensity of my preparation for my run at World's Strongest Man almost destroyed my marriage. Alex is right in the middle of Team Beast; she's the most important player on the pitch. Right at the beginning of taking on the fight, I spoke with Alex to figure out how we could avoid another blow-up. She knows I can't change who I am. I'd never want her to change who she is. She is everything to me. She keeps the whole show on the road

– cooking, cleaning, raising the kids, feeding me six meals a day, making sure I'm where I need to be when I need to be there. She deals with my business as well as running her own business, and keeps me on the straight and narrow in the good times and the darkest of times. I can't do any of this without her. It's that simple and I'll say it again – I cannot do what I do without her by my side.

Even at this preparation stage, my obsessive gene had kicked in and I was trying to identify the elements, the bricks that I needed in order to build my house of gains. The fact that it was one intense year of me living and training like a spartan and then it was done, was a huge factor in Alex getting on board.

Time is the one thing I can never seem to find enough of. We decided to have my training camp all on site in our home to make the best use of my time. In practical terms it meant building a gym in my basement and installing a boxing ring down there too. I already had a hot and cold tub in the garden outside, as well as my hyperbaric chamber. Pat moved into the guest house so that he was available twenty-four hours a day, seven days a week. It was a massive commitment from Alex and Pat towards my success. It was also a massive boost to my happiness and well-being. It meant that I didn't spend time travelling to gyms for workouts or spas for recovery sessions. I got more time with the wife, not much more mind, but every little bit counted. And they do say happy wife, happy life.

I always think, how can I build my life around whatever challenge I'm taking on, or goal I've set myself. Sure, it's a bit of commitment, but it's a commitment to making my life easier. Whenever I take on a challenge, there are always tough moments and plenty of hard work. But I always say, make the hard work as easy as possible.

As part of my preparation there were a few things I needed to face up to. One of Alex's fears was me getting injured or hurt in the ring. Personally, I didn't share her fears. Injuries happen. It happened to me in Strongman 2016; a stupid thing in the familiarization session ruined my chances that year.

But the other thing I had to confront was the possibility of losing. In a boxing ring with a beast and a mountain going mano-a-mano, one lucky punch could have ended it. That doesn't happen in Strongman, there's always the next event. But in this fight, it was one time and one opportunity. That's what made it so special. I knew I had nothing to lose. I had already won World's Strongest Man. I had already beaten Thor. I was getting paid a very nice amount of money to settle some scores in the ring with someone who wronged me. What did I have to lose? Instead, I decided I was going to enjoy it. I knew from my planning and preparation that there was a lot of graft in front of me. But my dream of getting into the ring with Thor was coming true. Life was pretty good!

After doing all of the sessions planning with Pat, I remember looking at all the sessions I had planned out all the way up to the fight. Every single one of them increased my confidence and my belief. I vowed to work harder than I had for World's Strongest Man 2017 and for that I was perfect for a year. By planning every session, I knew I would be perfect again preparing for this.

In 2016 I had never pulled 500 kilos off the floor. Yet here I was in front of 12,000 people in Leeds about to attempt to do just that. Pull 500 kilos. Smash a world record. Become a legend. No pressure then. How did I get here?

You might recall my story of the great Magnús Ver Magnússon disqualifying my world record deadlift in 2014. That was a pivotal moment for me. My fight or flight instinct kicked in hard in the aftermath and I almost walked away from Strongman altogether. I realized if I could harness the power of the fight instinct, I could use it to plot my ascent to the top of the Strongman world.

Despite having that power in my back pocket, the journey was still uncertain and there were many obstacles in my way. Not least my own depression. You know by now how obsessive I am when I set my mind to something. I wanted to win World's Strongest Man more than anything in the world, but I also knew I would never achieve it the way my life was at that time. I felt trapped in a life I didn't want to live, and I couldn't figure out a way forward. It was inevitable that depression would take hold. The disqualification of my deadlift world record was the final straw. Something needed to change. I had to find a way forward. Nothing was impossible.

In July 2014, after my disqualified deadlift, I called my

boss and I told him I wouldn't be coming into work for a while. I was suffering and I needed to get my head straight. A while out of work ended up being around six months. It was a period of time that allowed me to train as a professional Strongman without any financial worries. It felt like I could finally carry out the plan I had to become World's Strongest Man. I could train, eat and recover like a professional without any other distractions. I saw such huge improvements in my strength. More importantly, the depression lifted and I was so much happier. It felt like I was finally living the life I had been craving.

It was really that six-month period which allowed me to transition from a normal life to that of a professional strongman. I sat down with the union reps and my boss at the beginning of 2015 and they asked me if I wanted to come back to work. The honest answer was a resounding no. I did not want to go back to a life where I was working for someone else and I was trying to fit the things that made me happy around it. I took the redundancy pay-ment on offer and I poured that and everything else into becoming World's Strongest Man.

At that stage I knew I needed to have the money to

keep myself and the family for at least a year. The hardest part of being a strongman is not the training if you can believe that. Instead, it's earning enough to pay the mortgage and keep the lights on. I truly believed 2016 was going to be my year to win the title. As it turned out it wasn't to be but that's a different story I will go in to in more detail later. But it was in that moment that I started breaking down my goal of becoming World's Strongest Man into individual elements. I'm looking at all the bricks I need, totting them up, and I realize the house of gains I want to build is going to cost me quite a bit of cash. For example, diet alone is going to cost me a grand a month. I needed cash. There was a nice carrot dangling in front of me: an offer from Giants Live, a Strongman events organizer and promoter. They were offering a very big lump sum of money if I could do one thing – deadlift 500kg.

To give you some idea of the scale of the challenge in front of me, the world record at that point stood at 463 kilos. I know because I was the one who held it. After what happened in 2014 with my disqualified lift, I was determined to come back the next year and take the title of deadlift world record holder. I broke it in Leeds in 2015 and afterwards I said to the promoters, 'If someone were to come and pull 500 kilos next year, how much would you pay them?' After they finished laughing, they said to me, 'Name your price, Ed.' We agreed a deal and I announced it to the crowd at the arena that I was going to come back next year and break the 500kg barrier.

The 500kg deadlift was thought impossible in the strength and weightlifting world. For one, nobody was sure if the human body could even withstand that level of pressure on the heart and other organs. Even if it could, who was strong enough to lift that much weight?

I was very vocal about promoting the lift and my belief that I was going to do it. Pressure motivates me, always has, always will. By putting it out there across social media I was backing myself into a corner so that I had to do it.

As word spread, every single person connected to the weightlifting world said it was impossible. Giants Live, who were putting up the money, thought I was a nut-job. They didn't even think they were in any danger of having to pay out. Andrew Bolton, the first man to deadlift 1,000 pounds or 457 kilos, said it was impossible. Every day there were videos on social media by powerlifters and the other strongmen. Every single one of them said I was delusional, that a 500kg deadlift was never going to happen in their lifetime. It was impossible. My favourite word – impossible.

To be fair, it should have been impossible. I was aiming to add 37 kilos to the current world record. That's the same as Usain Bolt going out and saying he's going to knock a second off the 100 metres world record. That was the jump I was trying to make.

People thought all I lived for was training for deadlifts and being hydrated. Not true. At that time, I was training to win the World's Strongest Man – that was my only focus. The deadlift world record was a side quest that I pursued because the money on offer would allow me to train better for Strongman. If I could pull 500 kilos, my training costs up to Strongman 2016 would be covered.

Do you want to know a secret? Of course you do. In training I had never pulled more than 450 kilos. That was a fact. I had never even been close to 500 kilos. I suppose I had never wanted to approach that number because I was worried about the repercussions on my body. I wasn't sure if I could pick up half a tonne and survive it. How was I going to break the 500-kilo barrier without breaking myself?

Once again, preparation was key. I was already very close to the peak of my powers anyway given I was in the midst of my regime for World's Strongest Man. I came up with a plan that would help to prepare me both mentally and physically for the challenge. I needed to prepare myself physically in a way that would preserve my mental belief that I could actually make the lift. The plan I put in motion was to lift 90 per cent of my target lift of 500 kilos. For those of you less nimble of mind, that's 450 kilos. I said let's never go above that in training but let's make 450 look easy. Let's make 450 look like lifting a feather. I knew if I could do that, then when the time came to lift 100 per cent of my target, the 500 kilos, it would fly up. I kept consistently chipping away so that the 450-kilo lift was getting easier and easier. It got to a stage where, no joke, I was pulling 450 kilos as speed reps. I was pulling it quicker than I could get out of a chair. It was that fast. By approaching the challenge that way I preserved my body and I also preserved my belief.

A 500-kilo deadlift was a massive psychological barrier in the weightlifting world. The world record had only been moving up in increments of 1 or 2 kilos every few years. I knew preserving my belief that I could make the lift was almost more important than the physical preparation. If I had gone for 500 kilos in the gym and failed, my head would have fallen off and my belief would have been shot. If that had happened there is no way I would have broken the world record. I would have believed it was impossible, just like everyone else. But I've already said that for me, impossible is impossible, right.

So, it was crucial I stayed away from trying to lift half a tonne in training, but I couldn't avoid it forever. At some point in front of a screaming crowd of thousands I would have to back up my bull. How was I going to pull it off? I already had an army of specialists at this point as part of my meticulous preparation for World's Strongest Man. You name it, I had it – doctors, scientists, physiotherapists, psychiatrists, hypnotherapists, strength coaches. I sounded all of them out for advice on how to make the lift and make the impossible seem possible.

There was one scientist I spoke to who specialized in

strength. He explained to me how the human body recruits muscle fibres and how the body then relays that into movement. Your average person who takes his kids to school, does the shopping, goes to work, has access to about 50 per cent of their muscle fibres. An elite sportsman, someone who trains fifteen to twenty hours a week, has a little bit more, maybe 65 to 70 per cent of their muscle fibres they can recruit. But then he goes on to explain about scenarios in life. One might be a kid being trapped under a car and the mother trying to lift the car off the kid. They can recruit 100 per cent of their muscle fibres and that's down to the fight or flight scenario. Here was a scientist confirming what I already knew, something we covered in the last chapter – the fight or flight instinct is a superpower. The key to making the deadlift was triggering a fight instinct powerful enough to recruit 100 per cent of my muscle fibres when I needed them.

I consulted with a psychiatrist about what I wanted to do. I needed to trick my body into recruiting 100 per cent of my muscle fibres so that I could make a world-record deadlift. He told me I would have to go to a very dark place mentally to get the physiological response I was seeking. Together we crafted a scenario in my head that was absolutely horrific. It was seriously dark, far too dark to share with you here. The hope was that it would inspire the necessary fight instinct to recruit 100 per cent of my muscle fibres and allow me to make the lift. That was the hope, but we didn't know for sure if it would work and I wasn't prepared to test the theory in the gym in case it didn't. I was only ever going to attempt this lift once.

If you haven't seen the video of me making the lift it's worth a look. I still don't really know how I did it. I think I convinced my body that it was stronger than it was. In that respect it was as much a triumph of mentality as it was of physicality. The scenario I crafted to trigger my system into recruiting 100 per cent of my muscle fibres worked. You can actually see my eyes go black in the moments before I step to the bar. Then I did it. I demolished the impossible. I deadlifted 500 kilos.

The key to me lifting half a tonne was in my preparation. Mentally and physically, I went beyond what anyone had ever done before. More than breaking the world record, it was actually the methods I used to do it that I was most proud of. All of the elements were coming together in a way that set me apart from everybody else in the world. It gave me tremendous confidence to stay on the path I was travelling. From that perspective, the world record deadlift was a very important signpost on the journey if you like. The cash that I earned for the lift came in pretty handy too!

One of the things that was a massive help to me as I prepared to fight Thor was speaking to my allies. These are people who are on a similar journey to me, people like Ross Edgley, James Haskell and Paddy McGuinness. Ross is an author and adventurer, as well as personal trainer to the actor Chris Hemsworth. James is a former English rugby international who is now a DJ, podcaster, author and presenter. Paddy is an actor, comedian and TV pre-senter. He is the current host of *Top Gear* and *A Question of Sport* on the BBC. They gave me some brilliant insights on the challenges they faced in their careers.

I talked to my good friend James Haskell about pre-paration and process. James told me, 'You derive confidence from your preparation; being prepared gives you so many layers of benefit. It gives you the confidence to know that you put the work in, so when you come to compete, you've already done what you need to do. And then it's just managing pressure and delivering and executing the next thing which refines your process.'

This really hit home to me how important process is in keeping your head clear. And then James said, 'When I turned up to a game, I would make a playlist that I would use for a month and then update it. I would know as soon as I put my headphones on. I made a couple of notes in my notebook that I had on my phone about the goals I wanted to achieve. I was in game mode and nothing was going to disturb it. And that was how I did it. So everybody in all their sports has those kinds of shared things.'

There's something great here that James identifies which is about process. It's the bridge between visualization and repetition. Finding a process that works for you, that delivers success, is crucial. The process is what emerges from the planning, the visualization and the hours and hours of work that you put in. I want to highlight that to you because it's such a great point that James makes. The other thing that James said which I want to highlight, is that having prepared right and done everything he could in order to succeed gave him confidence. I'm the exact same way. I'll work my arse off; I'll leave no stone unturned in my preparation and because of that I have so much confidence that I'll deliver when the time comes. Two great points from James.

I also sought out the wise counsel of the muscle monk that is Ross Edgley. Ross told me a great story which illustrated how extreme challenges require extreme levels of preparation and commitment. Ross said, 'I'm brutal with the people who I coach and train about having no excuses. I'll say to them, 'If you don't want to train, then don't do it. But it's going to be so hard to accept when you lose that you didn't put in the hard miles.' I loved this point Ross made because it's about eliminating excuses. If you create a plan and you stick to it then you know you have done everything in your power to achieve your goal. Ross also spoke about his time training Olympic gold medal athletes like Linford Christie, Tessa Sanderson and Greg Rutherford to swim the English Channel. Ross said, 'They were amazing because a lot of them couldn't even swim to begin with. We had eight weeks to train them from not being able to swim, to swimming the English Channel. At week three, I remember asking Linford

Christie to swim at least 1 kilometre in pretty cold water in Lake Windermere. Remember, three weeks before he couldn't swim at all. Linford pushed back – he said it was stupid. The rate of progression was so quick. I agreed with him. I told him it was stupid. But this is what you have to do, otherwise the English Channel is going to completely humble you. It's non-negotiable. It's the same in anything you do. If you want to achieve it, here are the non-negotiable things you have to do. You can't miss a meal. You can't miss a training session. That has to be the mindset. The preparation has to be non-negotiable. Or don't do it, because you're just kind of half-assing it. If you're half-assing it, there's no point.' I couldn't agree with Ross more. The point I'm making to you is that you have to commit to your plan and the commitment is non-negotiable. You don't miss sessions; you don't skip meals. You do whatever it is you have to do to hit your goal.

When I put up the announcement of the fight with Thor on my Instagram you would not believe the responses I got. Every man and his dog reached out. It felt like anyone who had ever thrown a punch in their life wanted to train me for the fight. There were also some big boxing names who reached out and offered to help. I didn't want to do one session with them for their Instagram and then get pawned off on one of the club trainers. I was looking for someone who could step up and be a boxing mentor as well as someone who was ready for an adventure. This fight wasn't going to be like anything they had ever encountered in their career. I needed someone who lived and breathed boxing. I needed to be at a professional standard in less than a year and I had zero skills.

I also realized how important it was to me to have my training camp on my terms. I needed someone who was going to work around my routine and not the other way around. I needed someone from Stoke. I started asking around the local scene and there was one name that kept coming up. Lindon Newbon. More about him in the next chapter.

Key Learnings

- Fail to prepare properly, prepare to take a proper beating. This is what I really want to impress on you and for you to take away from this chapter. Victory or defeat begins with preparation. If there is a goal you want to achieve or a challenge you want to take on, the very best thing you can do to ensure success is to formulate a plan. Plans give you structure, they hold you accountable and they give you purpose.

- There's an old boxing saying – train hard, fight easy. I want you to think about how you can build your life around whatever challenge you're taking on or goal you've set yourself. I know it's a big commitment, but it also is a commitment to making your life easier. I'm assuming you're determined to achieve what you've set your mind to. You're going to have some really tough moments on your journey and it's going to be a lot of hard work. My advice to you is to make the hard work as easy as possible to do.

- When I prepared to fight Thor I made a plan. Every session in the plan, every little goal, was a brick. And as I put brick on top of bricks, I built a whole house made of gains. Each element gave me a slight gain, each brick made the wall higher and sturdier, but in itself it was not that significant. It was only when I put all my gains together, all my bricks, that I had this sturdy house. By doing it this way, it made all of the hard work I put in pay off in the most efficient way possible. I want you to think in that way when you come to making your plan. What are going to be the bricks that you'll use to build your house of gains? How can you put those elements together so that all the hard work you do pays off in the most efficient way possible?

- Accountability was crucial to my success. I applied myself to my goals, worked my guts out and held myself accountable. My advice to you is to create an environment where you hold yourself accountable to your goals.

- My heart was totally invested in what I was trying to achieve. It was heart that carried me through the hard days when I was struggling to get through a session. Commit with all of your heart to whatever it is you want to achieve.

- I was very vocal about promoting the 500kg deadlift and my belief that I was going to do it. Pressure motivates me, always has, always will. By putting it out there across social media I was backing myself into a corner so that I had to do it. Does pressure motivate you? Think about the ways that you can put pressure on yourself to achieve your goals.

- I knew preserving my belief that I could make the lift was almost more important than the physical preparation. Confidence in yourself and belief that you can achieve your goals are key. The person who wins is the person who believes they can!

ROUND 3

Find a Mentor and a Nemesis

Mentors and nemeses. The yin and the yang. The light and the dark. The good and the evil. I've run out of comparisons, but you get it. In an ideal world, a mentor brings out the best in us, and a nemesis brings out the beast. I knew if I was going to win this fight, I'd need both. I'd be an angel when it came to the prep, and a devil when it came to the fight.

I was dead lucky to have found an amazing mentor in Lindon. He has been around the fight game for over forty years training local prospects in Stoke for the professional fight game. What Lindon doesn't know about boxing ain't worth knowing. The best thing was, he was so generous with that knowledge. When we first started working together in the ring, I was very green. Lindon got me up to speed and had me feeling like I'd been boxing for years. It felt like Lindon had been a part of Team Beast for years. It was the perfect partnership; he slotted in seamlessly.

When we started working together, Lindon laid out a pretty savage challenge to me. By the time I faced Thor, Lindon wanted me to be at a level where I could live with any heavyweight in the world if I climbed into the ring with them. Now, I love a gauntlet being thrown down. And this one told me a couple of things about my new coach. Firstly, it told me that Lindon and I were on the same page when it came to the level that I wanted to get to. He didn't say, 'I want you to beat Thor.' He didn't say, 'I want you sparring with the really good lads down the boxing club in a few months' time.' He set the best in the heavyweight business as my target – he wanted me to have the skills to go toe to toe with the Anthony Joshuas and the Tyson Furys of the heavyweight boxing world. Secondly, by setting me that challenge, Lindon said one thing loud and clear: Eddie, I believe in you.

Lindon Newbon

So my impression of Eddie is: very focused individual, very intelligent individual. He's very driven. He's very easy to train because he is responsive. But he'll also challenge you. If he doesn't think that something is right for him, he'll question you. Sometimes we'll go back and forth. Sometimes he gets my point. Sometimes I get his point. I think that's the reason we're still together. It's a very, very open relationship. I trust him. And I believe he trusts me. So it works. And that's what you need in this sport. Because people say it's an individual sport, because there's only you and your opponents in the ring. But actually in the lead up to that, it's a partnership. And I feel that that partnership does work.

Strongman was a lonely journey for me in a lot of ways. Being an athlete was my day job and I was moonlighting by being my own coach. I plotted every single session of my year building up to World's Strongest Man, and then I had to go and do those sessions. By myself. It was thousands of hours lifting, thousands of hours of recovery and about 4.5 million calories. I had a team of specialists around me, but that's not the same as having a coach. A team of specialists don't come round your gaff and say, 'Right, Ed, this is what we're doing today.' But that's how it was with Lindon. It was a relief, if I'm honest, to be able to pass the responsibility of planning my sessions to him. It was one thing off my plate, and it allowed me to focus on getting better.

We did sessions almost every day of the week and he built me into a boxer from the ground up. Every session, Lindon was switched on and ready to go. I fed off his enthusiasm and intensity. Lindon is a proper professor when it comes to the science of boxing; we never did the same session twice. It was always different. The first few weeks of working together it was all about the footwork, the basics of how to move my body around a ring. Then we moved on to throwing punches – jabs, crosses, hooks. Finally, we started to put it all together, the footwork and the punches, as well as slipping shots and head movements. It was during these sessions I came to appreciate Lindon's attention to detail. During my sessions, Lindon was a monster for detail. He was like a hawk, watching my foot placements as I threw a punch. Was I off balance? Had I got my guard up? Was I ready to block or slip a shot and then counter? That was the beauty of working with a coach like Lindon. When I thought I'd nailed something, I had somebody there saying, 'Not quite.'

Lindon Newbon

I decided that we'd start right from basics. So we spent weeks and weeks and weeks on footwork drills, you know, with his hands in his pockets just to get his feet correct, his movement correct, his balance correct. You're dealing with a different thing with a man the size of Eddie. I train other heavyweights, but Eddie is a real heavyweight! He's a big man. The first thing was getting his balance, getting his feet working correctly. Then we worked on what we call shape, his stance and guard. We found that Eddie boxes with low hands, and people think that could be a mistake. It's not, because of the muscle mass that he carries; it's very hard and very tiring to keep the traditional boxing stance. So Eddie boxes with low hands. I was worried about that for probably a couple of sessions until we started getting people throwing shots at him. I very soon found that his reactions are so quick that it worked for him. He's throwing shots out of his opponent's peripheral vision. He was catching people with shots because they were coming from low. Whereas if Eddie had the traditional boxing stance for a big man, he might not have caught them.

The other thing is that Eddie is just so heavy and muscly, and over six rounds that will tire you. I train a guy named Nathan Gorman, who is at the top end of British heavyweight boxing. Nathan's got a traditional boxing style, completely different to Eddie. It's not one size fits all. We found Eddie's own niche. We went through all your basics – footwork, stance, guard, blocks, parries. We just did exactly what we would have done with any young lad coming through the amateurs, and just built it from there.

As I said, all of this was totally new to me. Having Lindon around was a completely new aspect of training for me. It fundamentally transformed the journey to my showdown with Thor. For the first time in my career, I had someone who was literally in my corner. Lindon's commitment to turning me into a boxer, his investment in my success, knocked me out. Which, when you think about it, ain't a massive surprise: he's in the knockouts business.

In a very short amount of time, we formed a real connection. I trusted Lindon 100 per cent, and that was no small thing for someone like me who has always been self-motivated and self-trained. Obviously, I was still completely self-motivated by this boxing challenge, but it was awesome to be able to rely on Lindon for a piece of my battle plan. I was not thinking about the plans for my sessions and my training all the time. With Lindon taking the lead on the tactical plan, I was able to work my backside off on becoming a better boxer.

Another thing that was new for me because I had a dedicated coach was that I now had somebody to talk to outside of training sessions. Lindon would ask me how I was feeling about training, where my head was at, how my body was recovering. We planned the next sessions together, we looked at what was coming down the road and prepared to run it over. Lindon is special and I knew we were building towards a special performance too.

But Lindon wasn't the first mentor I had in my life. There had been so many over the years who helped guide me through the challenges I faced. Thinking back to when I was a kid, my heroes growing up were in a way, my earliest mentors. They were the ones I looked up to and wanted to be like.

It's probably not that much of a surprise for you to learn that my first hero was the Austrian Oak, Mr Arnold Schwarzenegger. I was just a kid, and definitely far too young to be watching *Terminator 2: Judgment Day* (what a film!), but I guess that's what happens when you've got older brothers. I never forgot the opening scene where the Terminator rocked up to a biker's bar butt naked and started a fight with a gang playing pool. It blew my mind; he was bloody indestructible. He looked so cool riding off on a new motorbike, shotgun stowed in the side.

After that moment I wanted to be the Terminator. I still do. I got Terminator tattoos inked on my arm a few years ago. Google it. The tattoos were very special to me because they made me feel like I was indestructible too. I think it was a combination of the strength of the Terminator as well as my brother's reaction to Arnold's muscles that made me want to be like him. We'd never seen someone look that strong, and my big bro's jaw dropped. I wanted to be like that. I wanted people to look at me with their mouths hanging open. And there was something else that I remember, something beyond the Terminator character and Arnold's muscles. It was the presence, the charisma – nobody could take their eyes off him. He just had that special something that made him like nobody else. He was a star. Little Eddie thought, 'I'll have some of that, thanks.'

Without a doubt, when I saw him riding off on a nicked motorbike wearing a pair of nicked sunglasses, Arnold Schwarzenegger became a mentor to me. I told you already that I wanted to be so far from normal. Well, I'll tell you what ain't normal – being the Terminator.

Needless to say, I became obsessed with learning about him and where he came from. His mentality and mindset were, and still are, so inspirational to me. He has had a massive influence on me and I've learned so much from how he's lived his life. I've tried to incorporate everything I've learned from him into my own mindset. Arnold Schwarzenegger is a man who truly believes that nothing is impossible. He's a bodybuilding legend. Check out *Pumping Iron* if you've never seen it. After conquering the bodybuilding world, he set his sights on conquering Hollywood and smashed that too. I heard a story that when he was a kid, his local gym used to close at the weekend. Rather than miss out on two days of training, Arnold would break into the gym. At sixteen, he was already obsessed with getting bigger and better. A little matter like the gym being closed wasn't going to stop him from doing the sessions he needed to do. The level of commitment, the work ethic, the refusal to let circumstance dictate what he could or could not do; all that to me was awesome. He was obsessed. He said he used to feel sick if he missed a workout and that he couldn't look at himself in the mirror. Well, I know that feeling! Arnold had a vision for the life he wanted for himself, and he didn't let anything get in the way. And that became my approach.

He's still a hero to me today. I've been fortunate enough to get to know Arnold through the Strongman world and I've seen up close who he really is. Arnold is a person who gives so much of himself and his time to others. That's his philosophy, to give back. I find that very humbling and inspiring. The mentoring that started back when I was a kid has really progressed – these days we're in business together. I brought The Arnold Classic – a multi-sport event consisting of bodybuilding, strongman, figure and bikini competitions – to the UK for the first time ever in October 2021. I've learned so much from working with him. He's still obsessed – his work ethic and his enthusiasm are both inspiring and infectious. But it's not just the business side. He's almost a father figure to me, demonstrating how to live life with honesty, enthusiasm and integrity.

As the years went by, though, I had other mentors, too. It might surprise you to hear me say this, but I could never have won World's Strongest Man without Brian Shaw. He's about six years older than me and when I came on the scene, he was the undisputed alpha. He'd won World's Strongest Man three times and I was the new kid breaking into the elite club. It was obvious to me just how professional and clued in Brian was. There was a reason he'd won three titles. Straight away I latched on to Brian, hanging out with him, picking his brains. He didn't know it at the time, but he became my mentor as I transitioned from contender to champion. He showed me how to act on the Strongman scene, how to conduct myself, how to be a professional. For someone to open their heart like that to another competitor, a rival, was pretty amazing. I think it shows just how good-hearted and generous a person he is. Brian is the man I admire most in the sport, no question.

I've taken on Brian and Arnold's example and become a mentor to others. I've done training camps with the Stoltman brothers, Luke and Tom, who are from Scotland. We did a week-long camp where I showed them how I prepared for World's Strongest Man. I explained the reasoning behind all of those little extras that I did like physio and recovery. It really opened their eyes to how much work I put in. They've incorporated those elements into their training and Tom won World's Strongest Man 2021. I take a little bit of pride in his achievement.

I hope I helped him in some small way to improve and I'll be cheering him in every competition as he continues to dominate!

In 2021 I added the latest member to Team Beast, nineteen-year-old Josh Middleton. A gifted boxer, Josh stands at 6ft 10½in tall and weighs 18 stone. He was a very useful sparring partner as I prepared for the fight with Thor. During this time, Josh told me of his aspirations to go as far as he could in boxing. I believe his genetics and mindset can take him all the way. I decided to give this young man a chance in life and offered him a full-time wage to go and chase his dreams. He grabbed it with two hands, just like when I had that chance. At age twenty-six I was supported by a great man, my close friend Mo Chaudry who is an entrepreneur from Stoke, when I was on the brink of achieving my dream of becoming World's Strongest Man. Passing on that kindness when you can is important and it never stops.

Just as I did with Strongman, I immersed myself in boxing. I looked to the greats for inspiration and mentorship. Without doubt the number one fighter of all time is Muhammad Ali. I rewatched his fights and read up on how he approached each bout. One thing that bowled me over was just how brilliant Ali was in mentally approaching a boxing match. He had massive confidence and he was very vocal about what he said he was going to achieve. He delivered when he said he would and I love that. Would he be considered the greatest of all time if he hadn't? It's because he did what he said he was going to do; that's what made him the greatest.

Aside from his mentality, though, I watched how he moved in fights. How he was so ruthless when the opportunity presented itself to end a fight. Ali was an assassin in the ring. No movement was wasted, no punches were pulled, and I made a decision that I was going to try and be as ruthless as Ali when I got in the ring.

Nemesis. Rival. Enemy. It might surprise you, but Thor and I were once friends. When I first broke into the elite Strongman scene, Thor was one of the first guys to welcome me into the fold. It's a small community at that level. At any time, there are only ever five or six credible challengers for the title of World's Strongest Man. Thor and I were at the top of that group. We were there amongst the best strength athletes on the planet. The strongman scene is a bit of a travelling circus, so we would see each other many times a year at all these various events across the world. During that time, I got to know Thor's family, who are lovely people, and I also got to know the man himself. I've had him around for a barbeque in my house, if you can believe that. It's a good job I've got a big griller, because the two of us ate more than a couple of burgers and sausages that's for sure. When I think back on that era, there was always a competitiveness between me and Thor, and that's as it should be. We were two alphas competing for the title of strongest man on the planet.

We competed, we pushed each other hard, but at the end of the day we always shook hands and said fair play to each other. I have no problem saying that when I came on the scene, Thor was better than me. In a way, seeing somebody out there better than me was a help. When you're the best, you've got a target on your head. I know that from being the best, too. When you see somebody who is at the top of their game, it makes you say, 'Right, if I'm going to be the best, I'm going to have to work my guts out.' And so that's exactly what I did. I worked my backside off to get up to the elite level.

But as I got better and better, I noticed a shift between us. As I became more of a threat, Thor became more distant. He was a teensy weensy bit colder when he spoke to me. I didn't care, of course, because as far as I was concerned, we didn't have to be mates. But I think he was jealous of my development. I went from being the new guy to being a serious contender very quickly. I know for a fact he didn't like that I was breaking world records. How else can you explain the obsession to try and break my deadlift record for the last few years?

I bet it killed him to see my time come when I won World's Strongest Man in 2017. He had been competing in the finals since 2011 and at that point had never won it. In 2014, that was the first time I'd even made the finals, so to see me win just three years later must have been a right kick in the balls for him. But you know what? I don't care. I worked my guts out. I sacrificed so much. I endured hurt and disappointments. I persisted through two years of an obsessive training regime that almost cost me my marriage.

You're not entitled to win World's Strongest Man just because you've been born a giant. You have to put the work in. You have to suffer for it. Why do you think I won? I won because I put the work in, and I suffered for it. I won because I was the best of the best. I beat Thor fair and square and he couldn't take it. He was a sore loser. That's the truth of the matter. Rather than accept the loss, rather than look at himself and how he prepared for WSM 2017, he decided to sling mud at me and my victory. He decided to call me a cheat. In that moment, as I saw the true face of Thor, I saw the weakness in his eyes. And that was when he crossed over from being a pal to becoming a nemesis.

That was over five years ago. Like I said, the Strongman world is a small world full of big blokes. We've crossed paths since and I've always been super professional in my dealings with him. I set my own standards and I'd never allow myself to be seen as a bad sportsman. That's what mentors like Arnold and Brian showed me. I am always amicable whenever I see him. I'm a professional, and genuinely I just want to crack on and do my job.

So Thor, pal, if you're reading, and I'm sure you are, nobody will remember that you lifted 501 kilos in your home gym, and not in a competition. But everyone will forever associate me with lifting half a tonne. I blew past the limitations that you and everybody else had placed on themselves. I did it in front of 10,000 people, in competition. In the full glare of TV cameras and referees. Nobody disputes that lift. You lifted 501 kilos a full four years after I did it, at home without anybody officiating. Guess what, Thor? Nobody cares.

Thor has said he only took on that lift out of spite. He did it to discredit and destroy my legacy. If you ask me, that tells you everything you need to know about the guy.

This is what I mean when I say Thor is my nemesis. He brings out that competitive side in me; he brings out The Beast. When it came to preparing for the fight, it was not enough just to feel the support of my mentors in my corner. I needed to feel that fire of aggression and anger. It made me train harder, brought even more focus on my goal. There was something primal about two alphas getting in the ring to settle scores. It was Goliath versus Goliath.

While I used Thor for motivation sometimes, outside of that I didn't give him a second thought. I cared about the challenge. I cared about being the best. I loved embracing that competitive side of me. The fight allowed me to experience all of those things that I craved. It's why I dedicated one of the most precious things I have – my time – to it. I committed a year and a half of my life to becoming the best boxer I could be with all the sacrifices that entailed. There was something epic about what I did, and I felt that epic energy on my journey.

One upside of my success is that I've met people on a similar journey to me. The obsessives, the dedicated, the ones who are willing to sacrifice, the ones who place the pursuit of excellence above everything else. People like Ross Edgley, James Haskell and Paddy McGuinness.

I've been very fortunate to have been offered more opportunities since the World's Strongest Man win. I wanted it to change my life for the better and it absolutely did. I suppose one thing I didn't anticipate was finding so much common ground and forging friendships with so many people who I find inspiring. We are all on similar journeys, these allies as I call them, and we help each other along the way in any way we can. It's probably not a surprise to hear that we all share very similar mindsets. We're all striving to get a little bit better every day, no matter what field we are in.

Each and every one of these guys sets a standard that inspires and challenges me. Take Ross Edgley. He's like a mad scientist, trying to push his body to the limit and beyond. We talk a lot about training methods, diet, recovery, all the sports science nerd stuff. But we also talk about the more 'philosophical', if you want to call it that, side of what we do. Ross has this belief, which I think he pinched from a monk, about having to earn your happiness. Ross believes that the only way to earn your happiness is through suffering. Suffering positively, if you like, suffering for the right reasons. We've talked about this so much, probably because it underpins why we do the things we do.

I suffered for many years to win World's Strongest Man. And I suffered every time I turned up in the gym and had a big session on the pads preparing for the fight. But all of that hard work, the dedication, the sacrifice, the suffering, it's for something bigger, something that can never be taken from me, something eternal. It's not just the winning that I'm talking about, it's about the experience as well. The pursuit of your goal changes you. The journey to winning WSM, and the journey to this fight, has changed how I think about my life and what it can be. It made me realize how much I can achieve if I'm willing to suffer and endure. I suppose that's what makes having an ally like Ross so valuable. He gives me a deeper understanding of myself and my experiences.

Britain has the best boxers on the world stage and I'm proud that Anthony Joshua and Tyson Fury are two more allies who have been kind enough to share some tips and advice as I journeyed to the showdown with Thor. Obviously, it was very nice to have two of the biggest names in boxing to draw on for guidance and inspiration. They set the standard. I used that as fuel for my training too. People can laugh at me all they want but I set my goals as high as possible and I don't care what anyone else thinks.

In just the same way that I learned from Brian Shaw when I entered the Strongman world, I learned from those guys in the boxing world. I spoke with them about training, about diet and recovery. I was not going in cold to any of that sort of stuff but every sport tests the mind and body in a different way. I would have been a right idiot to not utilize all that know-how from two of the best in the business.

But there are lots of other people totally outside of the boxing world on whose support I drew. Paddy McGuinness is not a bloke that people might immediately connect me to. From the outside, we appear to be two very different guys moving in two very different worlds.

Paddy likes to work out and we were introduced via a mutual friend, bodybuilder and actor Martyn Ford. There are a couple of videos up on YouTube if you want to see the pain we inflicted on him. Through that, Paddy and I became acquainted, and I got to know what a top bloke he is.

He has become a good mate, and in lots of ways there are loads of similarities between us. We're both dads to young kids, we both work for ourselves, and he understands the unique pressures of being in the public eye. I've taken some steps into the TV presenting world with World's Strongest Man coverage, as well as fronting my own TV shows like *Eddie Eats America* and *The Strongest Man in History*. Just like it was nice to ask AJ about throwing a right cross, it's nice to have a mate like Paddy who has been doing all this TV stuff for twenty-plus years and is at the top of his game. I can ask him for advice and get his opinion on projects that are offered to me. He inspires me and makes me want to work even harder on my presenting skills. More than the professional stuff, he's become a really good mate to me, and I hope I am a good mate to him. It's so important to have someone in your life who you can talk to. They don't have to be big 'what is the meaning of life' conversations. Sometimes it's just about having a mate who you can ping a text to and have a laugh with.

I know I'm lucky. I've got a really strong group of people around me. My wife Alex, the most important person in the world, is my anchor and my rock. As I built up to the fight, I had Lindon and Pat in the boxing ring and gym priming me for the fight. I was lucky to have been able to call on a really amazing bunch of allies, including British heavyweight champions, for support and advice in the run-up to the fight. I know better than most that nobody can do it all by themselves.

Every day I'm grateful to have people in my life who challenge me, who tell me the truth and not what they think I want to hear. I have people who pick me up when times are tough and celebrate my successes when they come along. These people are my allies in life, the ones who support me in my journey towards my goal. I think about how I can help and support them with the challenges they are facing and the goals they want to achieve. It could be anything from a chat on the phone, to a training session together to cheering from the sidelines at some event. Whatever it is, I make sure I show up for them in the same way they show up for me.

Heroes, mentors and nemeses. All of them can help motivate and guide you to achieving your goals. I spoke with Ross Edgley for his take on who his nemeses are. He said, 'My nemesis is probably who I would be if I wasn't doing what I do. That other version of Ross might be sitting in a cubicle, working a nine to five. That's not who I want to be.' Ross's answer really resonated with me because I know what he means when he says his nemesis is the person he could be if he wasn't doing what he does. I had the same experience working as a truck mechanic when really all I wanted to do was become a professional strongman. Any time I'm feeling grumpy about work or my life I think about the life I could be leading if I had never pursued Strongman. That usually lifts me from my slump!

I asked Paddy McGuinness who his hero was as a kid growing up. Paddy said, 'My mum was the real hero to me when I was growing up. It was my mum who put the graft in. She fed me, clothed me, got me into school and instilled all the values I have today. My mum, she was my hero.' I think Paddy really encapsulates not only who and what inspires us but also what we all aspire to be – heroes that people look up to.

Key Learnings

- I want you to think of any mentors you've had in your life. How did they help and guide you through the challenges you were facing? You might turn around and say to me that you've never had a mentor in your life. I'd say that you're wrong. We encounter mentors all the time even in our earliest years. Who are your heroes? In many respects they are our earliest mentors, the people we look up to and want to be like.

- A nemesis can be a person or a thing which spurs us on to push us past our limitations. Who or what is your nemesis? Who is your Thor? It might be an opponent you want to beat, but it might also be a test you want to pass or a barrier you want to break. You might think it is impossible to overcome your nemesis. It's not. Overcoming a nemesis doesn't mean just winning; it's about improving yourself through a combination of hard work, sacrifice, dedication, consistency and self-belief. But the only real question is, how bad do you want it?

- Who is the mentor figure in your challenge or goal? Context is everything here. I immersed myself in the boxing world and trained like a professional. It was natural that Lindon, a professional boxing coach with over forty years' experience, became my mentor. What is your goal? If it's to run 5k or run a marathon, then speak to a running coach. If it's to go to university, seek out a teacher who can help you get the results you need to get there. If you're struggling with anxiety or to get yourself out of bed in the morning, speak to someone. The point is, whatever hurdles you face, it's okay to ask for help. More than that, it's crucial to ask for help. Nobody can do everything by themselves. It can be intimidating to reach out to someone who is an expert when you feel like a novice. Do it. It'll be the best decision you ever make. Mentors truly love nothing more than imparting their knowledge and wisdom to those willing to listen. So, keep your ears open and make sure you listen to them!

- Who are the people in your life who challenge you? Who are the people who pick you up when times are tough and celebrate your successes when they come along? These people are the allies in your life, the ones who support you in your journey towards your goal. Ask yourself who in your life is your ally? Think about how you can help and support each other with the challenges you are both facing and the goals you both want to achieve. In summary, make sure you and the people close to you support each other whatever way you can.

ROUND 4

Be a Lover and a Fighter

The 'why' behind things in life are worth a ponder sometimes. Why do I work my backside off? Well, I've always enjoyed the graft, even back when I was a kid. I clocked pretty early that nothing was ever going to be handed to me. But, I had a plan for where I wanted my life to go, and I knew it was up to me if I was going to get there.

I've also always been very vocal about the things I wanted to achieve and the goals I've set myself. I was that five-year-old who said he was going to win World's Strongest Man, remember? One of the things I've learned about myself is that I love pressure. I absolutely thrive on it. By being a loudmouth about what I wanted to achieve, it heaped massive pressure on me to back up my bull. Think about the deadlift world record. I put it out there pretty much anywhere I could. I said I'm going to do this knowing full well what the world's reaction would be. But more importantly, I knew what *my* reaction would be. If I put it out there, I knew that I couldn't let myself down. I think that's one of the great tools in my mental locker; I can pile the pressure on to myself and make things happen. Without a doubt, all my mouthing off helps me focus.

It's amazing how much the things I say seem to wind other people up. There's a lot of people out there who write me off as an arrogant so-and-so. I've read the comments! Well, let me say this to them. It's not arrogance when I say I'm going to do something and then I do it, is it? It's just stating a fact.

Why do people bite? Don't they realize every single comment that says I can't, or I won't do something, feeds my determination to prove them wrong. It's just another way of them saying it's impossible. All that negativity they send my way, that's like a mushroom to Mario – it makes me bigger and stronger. All the abuse, all the people saying I'll fail, I love that. All that chit-chat is just a gauntlet being thrown down. I love nothing more than backing up my bull.

But sometimes in life I've had to stare down a challenge that can't necessarily be resolved by hard work, or dedication or sacrifice. The year after I achieved my dream of winning World's Strongest Man, I was confronted with a lot of those kinds of challenges. As you know by now, to bring home the title, I had a very focused and structured approach. I formulated a plan in my preparation, and I executed it. But after I achieved my dream, the next phase of my life was much more undefined. The challenge I faced was how to best capitalize on my success and generate more opportunities from it. If you can believe it, that was a lot more difficult for me than speed-repping 450kg deadlifts.

The year after I won World's Strongest Man was a period of transition and adjustment to this new stage of my life. I said what I was going to do. I did it. And I was on to the next thing, the next adventure. I can remember one period where, between the TV shows, the seminars, the Q&As and whatever else, I hadn't been home for ninety days straight. I'd been folding myself into planes, and I mean literally yoga-style folding myself into planes, travelling the length and breadth of the world. I was staying in hotels, eating crap food all the time, with each day bringing me to a new city, sometimes two.

Now, I loved travelling, I loved trying new foods and I enjoyed meeting people, but between the ever-changing scenery and the intense grind, there was no downtime. It was full-on, full throttle work with twelve hours being the minimum shift I put in each day. I did ninety days of this in a row. And I did all of it without my family. No Alex. No kids. I reached a point where I just felt like I was . . . well, I was shattered. I could feel myself burning out with no prospect of any R & R to save me. I was hitting a wall in a major way, and I knew I had another forty days of the same treadmill in front of me. I had no clue how I was going to get through it.

The first block of work, my ninety-day sprint, finished in Florida. Unexpectedly, I had twenty-four hours off before I was due to start another forty-day cycle of new cities and more fast food. Straight away I was on to the websites looking for a flight to take me back to England. I had a window to get home and see the family and I knew I had to take it. It was a ridiculous trip in hindsight, but I was desperate to get back to see everyone, even if it was only for a few hours. I found a flight going to Manchester, and it gave me about fourteen hours at home before I had to fly back out to Colorado to begin filming a show for The History Channel.

I booked the flight and the day before my flight home, I did a session in the gym and I felt a pop and then complete agony in my right arm. I didn't know what I had done to it, but I was in bits. It felt like a hot poker was being jabbed down my shoulder through my entire arm. I spent the rest of that day taking painkillers and trying to get some rest.

There was no way I was missing my flying back to see the missus and the family, but I needed to get my arm seen to. In the airport I called a specialist back in the UK and he said he would make time to see me at short notice. In London. Of course, I'm flying into Manchester. So, my one and only day at home was spent travelling down to London to see if the specialist could fix me. He did a quick examination and then casually told me I'd torn my bicep off the bone. I asked him if he could reattach it.

The specialist said forget about it, you've lost your bicep. He gave me a prescription for painkillers, and I was sent on my way. That was ten of my fourteen hours gone. I had four hours with the wife and kids at home, then I was back on the plane, arm in a cast about to go into another forty days of intense work without a day off.

I remember sitting on that plane and thinking to myself, 'What am I doing?' I was so tired, I felt like a dead man walking. I was in serious pain, even with the painkillers. I hadn't seen my wife and kids for three months and when I travelled halfway around the world to see them I could only spend four hours with them. I was sitting on a plane bound for Colorado and I was staring down the barrel of another forty days of intense work. I had a moment where I thought to myself, 'Why am I doing this?' I seriously considered walking off the plane, walking out on the work commitments and just going and being with my family. Going through my mind at the exact same time was the thought that if I walked away from these opportunities, they weren't coming my way again. I knew there would be another winner of World's Strongest Man next year and he would be on this treadmill instead of me.

I was arguing with myself at this point and I thought, 'What have I got to prove to anyone?' If I wanted to walk off the plane and go home I could. I was injured, I was exhausted. Nobody would judge me for calling time and going home.

Nope. That wasn't right. There was one person who would judge me for throwing in the towel. And his name was . . . Eddie Hall.

I slapped myself across the face. I literally smacked and walloped myself with my good hand. What was I thinking? I had worked my guts out for these opportunities. I had lived like a monk for two years to win World's Strongest Man so that I would get these opportunities. Now I wanted to walk away from them? No chance. I realized this is what it's all about. This is what Ross Edgley meant when he was banging on about 'earning my happiness through suffering'. I knew I could get through forty days of graft even with one arm tied behind my back. I said to myself, 'I'll endure this and I'll come out the other side of it stronger.' I knew for a fact that once the forty days were done, I'd be delighted with myself. I had that moment of realization sitting there on the plane. I said to myself, 'Enjoy it, Ed. Enjoy these tough times because they are an opportunity for you to prove something to yourself.' It wasn't the forty-day cycle that was the challenge. It was how *I thought about* the forty-day cycle. It was down to how I had framed it in my head.

I knew my body could get through it, it was my mind I had to convince. I flipped my perception of those next forty days away from the negative aspects that I had focused on – being separated from my family, dealing with a serious injury and feeling exhausted. Instead, I changed how I thought about it. I reframed it as an opportunity and a challenge where I could show myself how resilient I was. I could prove to myself that I could still show up and do my job no matter the circumstances. I knew at the end of the four-month marathon stretch, I'd have a good whack of cash in the bank, and I'd have proved to myself that I could do it.

Once I focused on those positives, I'm not going to say that it was a doddle, but it became a whole lot easier. I still missed my family and my arm still hurt like hell. I had plenty of days that were still a grind and I was working my backside off. But you know what? There wasn't a single day where I wished I had walked off that plane and gone home. The temptation to quit was as strong as I've ever encountered, but I managed to resist it. So, what made me stay on the plane and not quit?

The answer comes back to the question I posed at the start of this chapter: Why do I put myself through what I put myself through? The truth of it is, I do it because I have to deliver for the people I love. I'm very fortunate to have a lot of people in my life who I love and who love me back. They are the ones who get me through the really hard days, like when I'm sitting on a plane feeling like I can't go on. I have to keep going for them. It's more than motivation, it's obligation, a sense of duty to deliver on my promises. I want to make them proud. I want them to say that's my husband, that's my son, or my brother, or my dad with tremendous pride.

The first time I experienced that desire to make someone I love proud of me was with my nan. We had a very close relationship. I'm not being unfair to my brothers, but it was obvious that I was her favourite. Any time I called round she lit up, all hugs and kisses. She spoilt me with her kindness, and she understood me in a way that nobody else did. At that time, I was a very aggressive, flamboyant and pretty much uncontrollable kid. My nan, for whatever reason, was able to completely calm me down. It was like she could flick a switch in me, and I'd become a different sort of kid. Looking back, I reckon what was going on was that I wanted to make her proud.

The relationship between a kid and their nan is always a special one. If there was anything on my mind, or if I had a problem I was struggling to deal with, my nan was the only person I could talk to about it. She passed away fourteen years ago, and it broke my heart to pieces when she did. In her final moments I made a promise to her that I would win World's Strongest Man one day. It became my quest, my obsession in that moment. I took on a responsibility to deliver on the promise I made to her. That promise became a proper source of motivation and it was one of the things that kept me going during some unbelievably tough moments. I believe she was looking down on me when I stood at the top of the podium after winning it. And I hope I made her proud.

While my nan was able to keep me on the straight and narrow when she was around, after she died, I went well off the rails a bit. I can hold my hand up and say I have put the people I love through hell. My parents, my brothers and my wife Alex have been with me through all the hardships, all the crazy stuff, all the lows. I felt an obligation to repay them. Especially Alex.

I met Alex during a very strange period in my life. I was in my early twenties and I had developed a very large chip on my shoulder. I had a lot of anger and, growing up in Stoke, I had plenty of opportunities to vent it. I spent my weekends getting into fights. I got a buzz out of it and in those few moments when I was throwing punches, I had an outlet for my anger. There were no end of blokes willing to fight me despite my size. Sometimes I'd end up fighting anywhere from six to ten guys at once. I always came out on top. I thrived on it; I was a one-man Fight Club during that time, but looking back, I wonder why I was like that.

I think growing up in Stoke played a big part in it. Around town you were no one unless you were hard. You were a nobody unless you could bang. And I could bang with the best of them. It was a currency in Stoke to have a reputation as a street fighter and I was notorious.

I find this completely ridiculous now looking back. It's funny how meeting someone can totally shift the way you think. When I met Alex, she changed everything. First off, she made me realize that it doesn't matter who hits the hardest. Nobody cares.

We very quickly fell deeply in love with each other. It was a bit of a thunderbolt for both of us, but we felt so at ease with each other. I felt like I could speak to her about where I saw my life going, what I wanted to do, what my dreams were. It took a certain level of vulnerability and trust to talk about those things with Alex. But I also never felt vulnerable sharing my vision with Alex if that makes sense. I was already training for Strongman events when I met her, but without doubt she sharpened my focus.

We moved in together six months after we met. We got engaged, married and had a kid – all pretty major life milestones – within two years. Alex became my anchor. There is the old saying that behind every great man is a great woman. But I would say Alex is the greater one out of the two of us. She bought into my dream and believed in me. It was her foundation, her support, her love that gave me the platform to pursue my ambitions. And I can say with absolute certainty that if I had not met her, I would never have won World's Strongest Man. Alex is my absolute everything. I owe my success to her, I owe my family to her and I owe my future to her as well. She is the rock; without her I would be nothing.

Alex Hall

What does Eddie mean, to me? He means everything to me. He's my whole life. I love him to pieces. He is my husband. He is the father of my children. He is my every-thing. We've built this life around us. I'm so grateful to him. He gives me something to do as well. It's not just about giving him something to do. I'm so busy, and that's probably good for me. I don't know what I'd be like without all that.

I suppose in summary, the bulk of it is cooking, and a lot of shopping, all the housework, all the kids' work. But to put it into perspective, because it's for Eddie, shopping for example, can't be something I do once a week. It has to be done every single day. I literally couldn't fit enough shopping in my car or in the trolleys to do it once a week. I'd look like a crazy person. So I go to Tesco at least once a day, and the staff all know me there. They're like, 'You're back again.' 'Yeah, I'm back again,' as I'm putting ten packs of salmon on the counter. They're looking at me like I'm a madwoman. Washing – Eddie changes his clothes with every training session. There's three or four loads of washing every day. Eddie's T-shirts aren't normal T-shirts, they are the size of a bedsheet. You try keeping up with that. It's just keeping the house going. We've got a big house; we've got a lot of things going on. Eddie's running the business from the house. Everything except for the gym work is what I do.

I think what people forget is that Eddie is more than just the guy that did the deadlift, or the guy that won World's Strongest Man. Eddie is a real person as well. He's got life commitments; he's got family commitments. He still has to clean his pants at the end of the day, and he still has to eat his breakfast, and he's still got a mum and dad and he's got a wife and he's got kids. There is a lot more to do than just a job.

Alex is not afraid to challenge me, to speak her mind, and to let me know when she thinks I'm talking nonsense. I think every relationship needs to have that space where one or the other can be devil's advocate. She is a very shrewd, very smart advisor and is really across the detail of all my business interests. She is *the* integral member of Team Beast and she's not afraid to call out the negatives when she sees them. I need someone like that, someone whose opinion I can trust absolutely.

I can say these crazy things like I'm going to sign a contract to fight a 7ft giant from Iceland, and she'll support me 100 per cent. I suppose it's an indication of how well we know each other and how far we've come on this journey together. She knows the drill; we've been through this before with World's Strongest Man. Alex knows what I'm like once I've committed to something and she just lets me get on with it. We are a team, a partnership and I know she's in my corner always. It's why I can't let her down, it's why I keep fighting even when I feel like I've got nothing left to give.

Alex Hall

I wasn't overly surprised when Eddie came to me and categorically said he was going to do the fight with Thor because he'd been dropping hints forever. And I know everyone's heard me say no boxing on the Eddie: Strongman *documentary.*

It's nothing to do with boxing. It's about losing him. But I kind of saw it coming because of little comments like, 'Oh, I'd love to get him in the ring and kill him,' or whatever. So, honestly, I wasn't overly surprised when he sat me down and said, 'This is what's going to happen.' And there's no point in fighting it. I've learned that with Eddie, I've been with him long enough. If he wants to do it, he's gonna do it.

It's kind of built in Eddie to do these things. I've learned how to work with them. I've learned how to keep him focused. I've learned what I can't expect of him and what I can expect of him. I've learned what he needs. I've learned a lot.

I'm well practised. I've had to do this before, but it's slightly different. There are differences in the training for boxing and the training for World's Strongest Man. I know Eddie, I know how he works, I know how his brain works. I know the commitment he's gonna put into it. I know that he can't cut any slack. So it's not like I've been thrown in the deep end.

Finally, there are my kids. There have been a lot of days when I haven't been there because I've been at a training camp or filming or competing. I've sacrificed a lot of time that could have been spent with them. How do I explain to my kids that I'm trying to build a better life for them? I hope when they are older, they will appreciate the sacrifices I've made to provide them with a better life. They have had to make sacrifices too. They haven't had their dad around for very long periods of time and that's a hard thing for a kid to have to deal with.

Also, my son, Max, has dyslexia, ADHD and dyspraxia. That's a lot for him to have to contend with. I've said before that money is the remedy to a lot of problems in life. It might not solve everything, but it's a decent start. I've worked my backside off for ten years to put myself in a position to earn big, like with the fight. I have to take that money off the table and bank it for them.

Why do I do what I do? Most of the time, I do it for my family. Parents, brothers, nan, wife, kids. They have shown me so much love, and they have given me so much support at times when I was at my absolute lowest. There are times when I want to sack off a physio session or I don't want to do a video for YouTube. There are times I don't want to get on a plane to go to an event. There are times I just want to hang out at home with my family. But I have these opportunities now that I could only dream about when I was working as a truck mechanic. I owe it to my family to squeeze every last drop of potential from myself and every last drop from the privileged position I'm in right now.

My experiences in my early twenties when I was getting into fights and generally being a nuisance are not unique. Lots of young men are like that. I think I was feeling a little bit lost but Alex sorted me right out.

I was lucky to meet Alex when I did. She helped to give me focus and we figured out what we wanted our life together to be like. The Strongman dream was already there within me. But it was Alex who bought into it and supported me in achieving it. She suffered just as much as I did. She put in the hard work and was just as dedicated to helping me achieve my dream. Alex got me through so many tough moments, and you'll remember I mentioned how she was there for me after my deadlift failure in Leeds. There were a million and one moments like that, and Alex was always the one who reminded me of the positives and kept me going.

Now, any time I'm feeling down, or I'm struggling to get through a session, I think of the people I'm doing it for. My nan, my parents, my brothers, my kids and, most of all, Alex. They are my ignition; they give me the spark I need to fire my motivation and help me to push through whatever I'm up against. They're the ones who I fight for.

Anything worth doing in this world requires hard work and, inevitably, hard work comes with a degree of suffering. Very few of us enjoy suffering, and yet I believe it is through suffering that we grow. That's true in the gym, isn't it? You don't get better at deadlifts by taking it easy on yourself. I was talking about speed-repping 450kg earlier. You think that's easy? Let me put you right on that. Speed-repping 450kg hurt. It was a whole of a lot of pain every time I did it in preparation for the half-tonne deadlift. But that pain was a step towards achieving my goal of breaking a world record. So I've learned, if I have to suffer, then I'll suffer for the people I love and for a life I love.

It's not just the gym, though. I've also been confronted with situations where I needed endurance, but not the physical kind. I'm talking about the mental fortitude I had to develop to pull through and out the other side. I'm talking about me, on that plane, on the verge of walking out on all the opportunities I'd worked so hard for. It was my mental strength which got me through that period. I reframed my situation. I saw it as a challenge to rise to, rather than a load of 'oh, hoo hoo, poor me' self-pity to wallow in.

For me it was straightforward – I was living my dream, I was doing work that I loved, and the work meant I could take good care of my family. I'd come so far, and I was willing to walk out on it all because I was having a hard time? Because I'd hurt my arm? Because I was lonely? I reframed those forty days as a way to prove something to myself. And I did. I proved that no matter what, I could crack on and get through it.

There have also been times I've been confronted with situations that I couldn't change, where no amount of graft was going to improve the situation. My nan got very sick with something that couldn't be cured. It's taken me a lot of time. It's taken years to be truthful, to make my peace with her getting sick and passing away. But now I can look on the positives of her life, this amazing woman, all that she was when she was with us, and the impact she continues to have on me. I still talk with her and I still make promises to her as I still feel like I can't let her down. Even when she was sick, she continued to be such a bright light in my life, despite all the pain she must have been enduring. There is no doubt she was, and continues to be, a massive inspiration. Now I focus on the lasting legacy of her life, the positivity she brought to me and all my family. It took me some time to see past my own grief and sadness, especially my anger at her being taken away. But I've learned from it. Sometimes I can't change situations, but I can choose to hang on to the positives and let go of the negatives.

When I'm going through tough times, as I sometimes do, I lean on the people who I love to support me. I lean on the people who I fight for and who provide me with the ignition when motivation is low. Those people fight for me, they pick me up and they help me through the hard times. I don't suffer in silence and I'm not afraid to ask for help. I know it's not weakness, it's a show of the greatest of strength. The fact that I've got people in my corner means that I have a good reason to get out of my corner when the bell rings, and never throw in the towel.

One of the key themes in this chapter is why I work so hard and what motivates me to do the things I do. Hard work and motivation go hand in hand. I know my work ethic can be traced to growing up as a kid. My parents were a shining example to me. I knew I'd have to work hard in the extreme to get ahead in life. I spoke with Paddy McGuinness about what it was like for him growing up in Bolton and how that influenced him. Paddy said, 'I was brought up around working-class people, living in terraced houses. There wasn't much money about. I was that kid who showed up at football and my boots were too small for me. They were always second-hand. I never had any of the right kit. That's what shaped me and made me the person I am. Those experiences gave me the work ethic to strive for more for myself.' This resonated massively with me. One of my memories as a kid growing up is of my mum breaking down at the petrol station because she didn't have the money to put fuel in the car. I've never forgotten that. It taught me the value of a pound I'll tell you that. Paddy and I had childhoods where we both learned the value of a quid. We learned to work very hard as a result.

I also spoke with James Haskell about his upbringing and how that influenced his values. James would say himself that he had quite a privileged upbringing in some ways. He said, 'I started boarding school when I was nine and I was there until I was eighteen. I was away from my family for very lengthy periods, but they were always present. My parents' commitment helped shape me into the person I am. They went above and beyond. They were never wealthy. They basically worked themselves to the bone, and they almost bankrupted themselves to put me and my brother through school.' James saw and appreciated how hard his parents worked to give him opportunities in life. That rubbed off on him and taught him the lesson that if you want something in life you have to work hard for it.

Parents and family are so important. It really struck a chord with me what James said about his parents and how much they sacrificed for him and his brother. My folks were always there for me and my brothers. Now that I'm a parent myself, I really want my kids to look up to me in the same way that I look up to my parents.

Key Learnings

- I want you to begin to think about what motivates you and why you do the things you do. It might not be your style to say you're going to do something before you do it, but it makes you more accountable to your goal. None of us wants to lose face or be seen as flaky or not able to follow through. Saying your goal out loud to other people might make you feel uncomfortable. Nobody likes stepping out of their comfort zone but it's a necessary part of the journey too. I think it's pretty much undeniable that it'll make you work harder to try and achieve what you said you'll do. I urge you to give it a try; you might even surprise yourself and find that you enjoy the pressure too!

- Have you encountered moments of wanting to quit? What did you do? Were you able to find a reason to motivate yourself and keep going? If not, why do you think that is? I have used my relationship with people closest to me as motivation in the hardest times. My desire to make them proud and to be able to provide for them got me through a very difficult time. Who do you want to make proud? Whatever journey you're on or challenge you're facing or goal you want to achieve, you'll find a deep well of motivation in making the people you love proud.

- Do you have a dream? Do you have a vision for what your life could be? What do you want from your career? What do you want from your life? These are big questions, and they require thought and reflection. Chances are you have some big dreams in your locker, but you're scared to reveal them because you feel like you might be judged or people around you might use them to put you down. If there is anyone who isn't on your side or makes you feel like you can't achieve a goal or a dream, then you don't need them or their negativity in your life. Dream big, achieve big!

- I want you to think about the relationships in your life and what they mean to you. Who do you fight for? Who do you want to make proud? Who do you feel like you have an obligation to deliver for? Who is your ignition? Love is an emotion that you can harness to power you through pretty much anything in life. I do believe we earn our happiness in this life through suffering. Any endeavour of real value requires hard work and inevitably, hard work comes with a degree of suffering. Very few of us enjoy suffering, and yet I believe it is through suffering that we grow. It is through suffering that we take those vital steps towards our goal or our dream. It is through suffering that we attain true happiness.

Setbacks Are Signposts to Success

My Strongman journey started as a dare. My brother Jamie loved to mug me off saying, 'You might have beach boy muscles but how strong are you really?' I was nineteen at the time and had been putting in the hours at the gym sculpting my physique. I knew I was strong, but Jamie had a point – how strong was I really? Jamie came across a novice Strongman event taking place in an industrial estate in Burnley, which is about as far from a beach as you can get. Jamie dared me to enter, which he knew was as good as a guarantee that I would do it. Being a complete novice, I had zero experience when it came to events like the Farmer's Walk, which involves carrying two giant dumb-bells of 160kg each over a set distance; or the Truck Pull, which is pulling a truck of 453kg over a 21-metre course. I still managed to finish fifth though. That was in 2007. After that, the Strongman bug bit hard. By a bit of a fluke, I found something that I had real talent for, and I was obsessed with getting better.

It took me ten years to ascend to the summit of the sport. At every step in my journey there were failures and setbacks. At times, the only way I made progress was through learning from my mistakes and losses. Those were the experiences that taught me the most about myself and, in their own way, showed me the direction I needed to go if I wanted to succeed.

I've had to learn to grudgingly accept failure as part of the journey to improvement. That's not to say I enjoy failing. It's incredibly frustrating to dedicate myself to something and to sacrifice time with the family only for it not to come together.

I had been working for about six months with Lindon on my boxing skills when I felt like I hit a bit of a plateau in early 2021. I knew this kind of thing could happen, especially with something as complex as boxing. In order to put in a cohesive performance it requires a number of different elements to come together. For whatever reason, with my boxing training, it was just not happening for me.

But I wasn't worried. I had been here before. I knew it could happen. I also knew that the key to overcoming it was to stay positive and keep grafting. During this period, I reminded myself that any failures I had in training were both helpful and temporary. They were helpful because they focused me on what I needed to work on. And they were temporary because I knew that in one week's time, two weeks' time, one month's time, I would crack it. Why did I have such faith? I knew the power of hard work. I knew that the only way to bridge the gap between success and failure was through hard graft. And I have never minded a bit of hard graft.

I used to take any temporary failure way too personally; it was a real ego-bruising exercise. I got so caught up in the loss that I failed to appreciate the learnings. But everything changed for me when I had a conversation with a sports psychologist about failure. They asked me a very simple question – what if I told you that you had to experience ten failures before you won World's Strongest Man?

For me, that was a light-bulb moment. In a very simple way, the psychologist was showing me how to rethink my experience of failure. The way I saw it, I had a choice; I could view failure as either a positive or a negative. If I viewed it positively, I could accept all the lessons from failure, rather than getting too caught up in poor old Eddie's hurty-wurty feelings. If I couldn't achieve something, rather than getting pissed off with myself, I made sure I was doing everything that I could to learn from my failure and improve.

It might surprise you, but I can be a pretty emotional guy, especially when it comes to my Strongman career. Think back to that story I told you about the time I pulled a world record deadlift, only for it to be disqualified because I didn't return the bar down to the ground to the judge's satisfaction. My response then, totally reasonable as I'm sure you'll agree, was to quit the sport. I thought to myself, 'Sod it! It was only seven years of hard work and sacrifice – time to pack it in and walk away.' It's fair to say that emotion clouded my judgement and decision-making.

It was Alex who showed me what had really happened, without all my emotions messing up the picture. I'd pulled more weight off the floor than any person in history had ever done before. I'd broken a world record even if it wasn't going to count over a technicality. I learned that you've got to jump through the hoops even when you're the best. Maybe especially when you're the best, because there are more people than ever trying to tear your achievements down. What happened when I pulled the 500kg deadlift world record? I made sure I wasn't disqualified for some technical nonsense.

Nearly quitting the sport I loved was an extreme reaction. It was me throwing my dumb-bells out of the pram because I was annoyed and upset. It illustrates how I let my emotional reaction to failure cloud my judgement. It was exactly this kind of thinking that the sports psychologist was trying to get me to change.

What the sports psychologist helped me to realize was that every setback and every failure is a sign that I was doing the right thing. It was a right head melt for someone as competitive as me to take that lesson on board. I was obsessed with winning but of course bitter experience had taught me I couldn't win every time. But rather than get wrapped up in the negative, I had to ask myself what positives I could take from the times I failed or from the setbacks I experienced?

It took me ages to be able to separate my emotions from the outcomes. Once I did, I began to appreciate that all my failures had something to teach me, and that made me so much better. I learned that it's one thing to perform a lift in a gym in training, but it's quite another to do it in competition in front of a screaming crowd. Every time I failed in competition, there was a value in the failures. For one, I was gaining competition experience which is impossible to replicate in training. I knew if I wanted to win World's Strongest Man, I would have to do it at a two-week event in front of thousands of people. The more exposure I got to that type of environment the better. If I made mistakes under pressure in a competition environment, then those mistakes provided an opportunity for me to learn to get better.

The final lesson I learned from the question the sports psychologist posed to me was to focus on my quest. At this time, my obsession was winning World's Strongest

Man. If I was stewing over a second place finish at Europe's Strongest Man or third place finish at Giants Live, it was not really of any value to me. Once I had identified the lessons to be learned from my performance, it was best to put the emotion of the loss to one side and move on. I shifted my focus on to the next event, and I never lost sight of my quest – winning World's Strongest Man.

I've learned to make failure work for me. I applied that mindset to failure during my fight preparation. I accepted that things weren't always going to go my way 100 per cent of the time even when I had put in the hard work. There were many sessions with Lindon where I failed, where my boxing was not coming together for me. The most important thing during this period was that I kept my mindset super positive, and I kept believing in myself. I never got discouraged, and I always used any setbacks as motivation. I made sure I saw any setbacks as signposts that directed me towards success. Of course I got frustrated at times, but it was a failure wasted if I didn't take the experience, dust myself off and learn from it.

I've realized that there is a difference between a setback

and a failure. Failures are pretty well defined. If I'm participating in a competition, I win or I lose. Simple as. If I lose, I can look at why. If I win, happy days. But whatever the outcome, it's usually pretty clear what I need to work on and how I can improve. Setbacks are different. They present a different sort of challenge and they test me in a very different way.

Injuries are some of the hardest setbacks I've had to deal with during my Strongman career. I've had some horrendous injuries through the years – tearing muscles off the bone, snapping tendons. Even something as simple as a muscle tear meant at least twenty-one days' recovery time. Training time was lost and mentally it was so deflating. I was my own worst enemy in that respect. I kept thinking of all my rivals getting in extra training sessions while I was stuck having to rest up. Even when I've been injured, or when I've faced any other sort of setback, there are lessons I've learned.

My most difficult setback occurred during World's Strongest Man 2016. It happened at the familiarization session which always takes place the day before the main event. There was a barrel being used for one of the events that appeared a little bit awkward to pick up, so I wandered over for a closer look. I flung it up on to my shoulder and as I did, I snapped the ligaments in two of my fingers. The left hand swelled up immediately and the pain was so intense. The medics took one look at it and told me there was no chance of me being able to compete. One year of preparation demolished in one moment.

It mentally destroyed me. On the back of the medic's advice, I told the organizers and the referees that I was out. I was absolutely devastated. My 2016 World's Strongest Man was over before it had even begun. I went back to the hotel room and phoned Alex to tell her the news. Once again, her reaction was probably not what I was expecting. 'What are you on about, Eddie? You've done yourself a booboo and now you're not going to compete? I've taken care of everything else for the last year while you've been training your backside off. You're going to let two sore fingers stop you now? The only way you're not competing is if you can't stand. Get back downstairs and tell the organizers and the referees you're back in.'

Alex, as always, told me exactly what I needed to hear. She was right. The fingers were damaged but that didn't mean I was not able to compete. My stress and anxiety cleared. The stand-by who thought he had my place was gutted when he saw me appear back down in the courtyard, but not as gutted as I would have been if I'd got on a plane to go home. I told the organizers and referees I was back in and I was going to compete. My grip was pretty much gone in one of my hands, which was a bit of an impediment when I was competing in events that required me to grip and lift hundreds of kilos at a time. It was a major struggle to get through some of the rounds. I've seen a video of me from it where I'm doing the circus barbell, which is a floor to chest lift and then a press overhead. I think around the eighth rep, tears began to stream down my face. I wasn't aware of it, but the silent cry was my body's reaction to the pain and stress I was placing it under.

I finished third that year. I was the third strongest man in the world with one arm tied behind my back. There were two ways I could have looked at that result. On the one hand, it was a tremendous result given the injury and the turmoil in the twenty-four hours before the competition began. But the other view was, I'd gone in as one of the favourites to win, I'd trained like a machine, and I'd come up short. It took me a little while to think about my performance without emotion, and only see the learnings.

I had been so confident going into 2016. I was certain I was going to win, and in my head, I had already spent the prize money. I arrived in Africa a few days before the competition to get used to my surroundings. I was eating well, I was sleeping well – I felt amazing. I felt ready to demolish the competition and I was excited to finally bring home the trophy. Then the injury happened, and it completely broke me. I couldn't sleep. I struggled to eat. And of course, the nerves kicked in. They were so bad I got sick before a couple of events. After I got back home to Stoke, I sat down and asked myself, 'What could I learn from my injury and the effect it had on me?'

The injury was one of those godawful random freak things that can happen. I wasn't cursed, the universe wasn't out to get me, but there wasn't a thing I could have done to stop it from happening. I picked up a barrel and I ripped the tendons in two of my fingers. The injury was something beyond my control, but what I could control was how I reacted to it.

It was uncharted territory for me. I was injured in the hours before the biggest competition of my career, and I panicked. I did the one thing you should never do in a crisis. I allowed my worry and stress, my emotions, to influence my decision-making rather than taking a step back for a minute and processing what had happened to me. I have massive respect for the medics, and I value their opinion very much. However, the decision to participate in an event as important to me as World's Strongest Man was my decision to make and mine alone. I should never have allowed myself to be swayed by their opinion. Thank God Alex was there to once again provide me with her wisdom and the kick in the backside I needed.

Getting through World's Strongest Man 2016 was such a struggle. Every morning I woke up miserable. I wasn't sleeping because I was so stressed out and I wasn't eating for the same reason. No sleep and no food made Eddie a very irritable Beast. I had to go to my deepest depths every single day to summon the resilience and courage I needed to get through each event. It felt like everything was against me. On paper, I had no business even attempting to compete. And yet I found a way to get through the pain, through the physical barriers and the mental doubts. At the time it wasn't great. I had to endure so much pain in order to even compete. But a few months down the line when I looked back on it, I realized that what I had endured was a masterclass in resilience training. That tournament taught me so much about myself. I knew that I could push through no matter how hard it got. Coming third was an achievement in the circumstances but there is no doubt in my mind that I could have won the title in 2016 had I stayed free of injury. The experience, as much as the injury was a setback, really did give me tremendous belief looking ahead to World's Strongest Man 2017.

The final gift of my injury setback was anger. I had put so much work into 2016 and for injury to derail it all on the day before the event made me furious. And I used that anger all the way through 2017. The fury fuelled my obsession and there were never any shortcuts in training, in recovery or in my diet. I didn't miss one of my gym or recovery sessions all year; everything was on point. The setback in 2016 made me even more determined to ensure that 2017 was going to be my year.

The injury at World's Strongest Man 2016 was a random event over which I had no control. The only thing I could control was how I reacted to it. In the first instance I panicked, and I made a poor decision to drop out. Thankfully I had the conversation with Alex to give me the perspective I needed to make the right decision. The whole experience taught me to never make a decision when you're panicking. There's a lot to be said for taking a moment to sit on your hands when something bad happens. Of course, I felt very overwhelmed when I did my injury. But with Alex's help, I was able to adjust to the circumstances and I found a way to keep moving forward towards my goal. I think that's the key to resilience. It's finding a way to keep moving forward, no matter the circumstances, no matter the obstacles, no matter the pain. I must find a way to keep on towards my target. That's resilience in a nutshell.

I've realized that so much of success is failure. The most important part is to not let failure have the final word. Try, try and try again. Keep positive, even if you have to crawl. That's what success is made of.

Every epic journey has twists and turns, and my

Left: Eddie (Age 5) with eldest brother Alex on holiday in Portugal.

Below: with Mum (Helen), Dad (Stephen) and brothers Alex and James on holiday in Portugal.

Eddie Hall aged 21, Northwich Strongest Man.

Above: Eddie on the podium at World's Strongest Man 2017.

Right: Eddie with his World's Strongest Man trophy 2017.

Below: Eddie deadlifting 500kg/1102lbs for the World Record.

Above: World record deadlift 462kg at the Arnold Classic Melbourne (Australia).

Above: Eddie posing with his idol Arnold Schwarzenegger.

Right: Eddie with wife Alex at a Charity Gala in London.

Eddie training in the gym.

Eddie with wife Alex and son Maximus
celebrating Eddie's 34th Birthday.

Above: Flying out to World's Strongest Man 2016 with fellow competitor Brian Shaw.

Left: Eddie doing a serious photoshoot.

Below: Eddie and Brian at World's Strongest Man 2021.

Eddie and Thor competing at Europe's Strongest Man 2017.

Eddie, Brian Shaw, Nick Best and Robert Oberst sitting in Paul Anderson's house filming *The Strongest Man in History* for the History channel.

Eddie and Pat Gale during the fight camp 2020.

Right: Eddie and Lindon out in Dubai – fight camp 2022.

Eddie during boxing camp 2021.

Above: Eddie and Arnold Schwarzenegger – business meeting in Wales.

Left: Eddie with his son Maximus.

Below: Eddie training with Ross Edgley.

showdown with Thor was no different. I threw a lazy hook in sparring, twelve weeks out from the original date for the fight and I tore my bicep off the bone, the other arm this time. The mood in my camp was like a morgue when it happened. Once I had time to come to terms with the injury and get it assessed, I moved on to the next goal – coming back better and stronger. I got myself down to Harley Street in London the next day to have the injury seen by the best doctors. I needed surgery, but they said I was lucky. It was only a tear of the tendon. There were no bone fractures or anything like that, which made it a much more straightforward operation. The surgeon said that the tendon had probably suffered micro-traumas for years and years due to my Strongman career then all of a sudden, it gave way.

If you've seen it on YouTube, you know the medics kept me awake during the surgery. Without any pain meds, I was expecting a scene out of *Hostel*. But you know what, the whole procedure wasn't painful at all. The doctors were super happy with how it went, and they encouraged me to start rehabbing a few days after the operation. That's what I did. Building back super slowly was frustrating in the short term, but I knew it was the only way to secure my goals in the long term. Obviously, the injury was a massive pain, not something I wanted to go through, but I had been there before. I used the experiences of tearing my other bicep off the bone, and when I injured myself before World's in 2016, to reassure myself that I would come back stronger from this injury.

Life is always teaching us a lesson. I've realized that so much of life is failure and setbacks. The most important part is to not let failure or a setback have the final word. Getting knocked down is inevitable. How quickly you pick yourself up again is what counts.

If there's a failure that still rankles, it's the log lift world record attempt in 2018. This might surprise you but I didn't want to attempt it. I had been very clear after winning World's Strongest Man in 2017 that I was retiring from competition. I had given everything to the sport, I'd conquered my dream and I wanted to move on with my life. The truth of it was that Strongman wasn't ready for me to move on. I was the biggest draw in the sport at that time. Every professional sport is also a business, and it depends on punters coming through the doors and attending the events. Early in 2018, promoters pressured me to commit to attempting a world record log lift. I probably felt a bit of an obligation to Giants Live, who had been very good to me through the years. There was also a lot of chatter from the other athletes and from fans across social media calling for me to come back and compete. Things I'd said in the past about what I wanted to achieve were wheeled out and it got to a point where I felt I had no choice but to back up my bull. This time, though, it was a mistake.

I had spent time away from the gym enjoying my win but now I had to knuckle down and get back into training for the world record attempt. I was feeling pretty confident that I would be able to add another world record to my name. Two weeks before the event I was coming out of my mum and dad's house when I stepped on a doormat, bang, and snapped my ankle. It was a bad injury, but I'd said I was going to try for the record, so I battled through the pain. I strapped up my ankle, pulled the foot into a tight boot that supported the injury and I just carried on. I did my training in the gym. It was agony, but I found a way to get through it. I knew it was two weeks of pain and after I'd competed, I could rest the ankle properly and give it the time it needed to recover.

I get to comp day and the ankle was in a pretty bad way, but the event was a sell-out and I couldn't pull out at the last minute. I strapped it up and made my way to the arena floor. The reception was overwhelming; the crowd really let me know that day how much they supported me. It was a special moment and it felt like a recognition of all of my years competing in Strongman. Unfortunately, as you know, I wasn't able to deliver a last world record for them. I got the log above my head; I locked my arms. I went to bring my head through to show the referee I was in control and get the down call from them. As I did that, I put all of my weight on the good ankle and the whole thing fell apart.

I never got the opportunity to put that failure right. Part of me wishes that I could have tried to do it again the following week. Maybe the ankle would have been in better shape, and it would have been able to take more of the load. Maybe I never would have made the lift. I don't know, and I'll never know now.

There were a couple of things I learned from this

experience. Firstly, I should have listened to my gut. I had said I was retired from Strongman events and that my competition days were behind me. I should have stayed retired. I felt a little bit pressured to do something that I knew in my heart I didn't want to do. I should never have allowed the pressures of the promoters, competitors or the fans to get to me. I should have stayed true to myself.

The other lesson I learned is that I can't win them all. I suppose knowing that requires a certain level of humility and acceptance – maturity, in a word. I'm not great at any of those things. I'm obsessive, and any setback feeds my obsession and drives me on until I succeed. Maybe if I felt I had something to prove to myself and to others in the Strongman game then I would have got back in the gym with the focus on making a world record log lift. But I didn't have anything to prove. I'd gone to the World's Strongest Man in 2017 and I had dominated. It was my pinnacle. Did I really want to go back into the gym and train to break a log lift world record? The simple answer was no. I wanted to get on with my life. I wanted to set new goals and experience new things. My failed log lift confirmed what my gut already knew. The Strongman chapter was over.

There is an art to knowing when to walk away. It is a combination of timing, intuition and self-reflection. It was my time to move on and chase new things. There is a serenity too, in knowing when to let something go. I'm certain I walked away from the Strongman world at the right time.

There was no serenity when I faced down Thor in the ring. It was so primal, the two of us going to war with each other, each trying to knock the other out. It was a real mental shift from our rivalry as strongmen. In Strongman we were trying to outlift each other, but in the ring we were trying to punch each other in the face until one of us was knocked out. As boxers we both knew there was nowhere to hide, which brought with it serious pressures.

As I reflected on setbacks and failures, there was one final question I asked myself. How many opportunities did I get to achieve my goals? It was worth thinking about. I didn't have the definitive answer, but I reckoned the truth was that I didn't get all that many chances. I had six goes at winning World's Strongest Man before I eventually brought it home to Stoke. How many more attempts would my body have allowed me if I had failed in 2017?

The weird contradiction is that I have learned far more from my failures than I ever did from my successes. Still, it's a question worth considering. How many shots will we get in life to succeed? We work very hard; we sacrifice so much and we fail a lot. We mostly fail in fact, which is why it's so important to seize the opportunity to succeed when the stars align.

Alex Hall

I do think it would be silly to consider anything Eddie does to be a failure. I think if I do ever say anything to him that helps, that's just my opinion. He has done so much. He can't fail at anything at this point. It's also a case of looking at the bigger picture. All right, so something you want to do hasn't worked out this time. You didn't do what you set out to do. But look at what you have done. Look at who you've got behind you. I'm here. Your son is here. It's just those kinds of things I think Eddie needs reminding of every now and then. Eddie's so busy looking forward, looking at the next thing he wants to achieve. If it doesn't work out, he thinks it's a massive loss, but it's not. He just needs his eyes opening a bit to look at the bigger picture, to see how much he has achieved and how much he still can achieve.

This round is all about failures and how I learn from them. I was really interested to speak with my team of allies about their experiences of failure and what they learned from it. James Haskell told me how he learned to deal with failure. 'I was very hard on myself and very self-critical. I had to go and see a sports psychologist early in my career when I was eighteen. I built a team to help me deal with failure. When I failed, I tried to take the learning from it. I also learned it's really important to surround yourself with good people who are going to give you genuine feedback. You need somebody to point you in the right direction and tell you how to improve.'

I know how lucky I am to have Alex in my corner. She's the one who has always helped me to keep my failures in perspective. She's also always been on hand to say just the right thing at just the right moment.

Next I spoke with Ross Edgley about failure and how he uses it as a source of motivation. Ross told me about a swim he attempted for charity. 'There was one swim that I did between Martinique and St. Lucia in the Caribbean, 40 kilometres from point to point. I did that pulling a 100-pound tree, which was for ocean conservation and deforestation charities. I ended up swimming over 100 kilometres because of the tides. I was in the water for over thirty-six hours, and I got so close to the shore that I could see the cars. Then I got caught in a counter current and was pulled way back out to sea. At that point my support boat pulled me out of the water against my will. I was very dehydrated, completely exhausted and not making much sense. The team got me rehydrated and back to my senses on the journey back to the hotel. I knew I'd failed. I felt almost physically sick at the realization. It was horrible; I've always been a terrible loser. I remember saying to myself, "I never want to feel like this again, ever. I'll do anything to make sure I never feel like this again."

'That experience has been a tremendous well of motivation for me. The fear of failure drives my process which is meticulous in detail. I'm looking at everything, leaving no stone unturned, planning with military precision. Then the outcome almost becomes inevitable because I've trained so hard.'

I can really identify with what Ross is saying about using failure as a motivator to improve and get better. It's interesting how failure can help you to think about improving your preparation and adjusting your process until you hit the goal.

Key Learnings

- What is your attitude to failure? Can you think back on a time in the past when you failed? What was your reaction? Did you double down and commit to working harder? Or did you allow that failure to discourage you?

- Have you ever let emotion cloud your assessment of your performance? Have you been so caught up in the failure that you've missed the positives you could take? It's easy to get lost in the pain of failure or in the frustration of a setback. But you have to ask yourself how is wallowing in those emotions helping you to achieve your goal? It's so important for your progress to detach from the emotion and be able to critically assess your performance if you are to learn the lessons that failure offers!

- I want you to think about the failures you've encountered in your life. How can you reframe your most recent failure as a positive which you can learn from? How can you use what you've learned to help you ultimately achieve your goal? Whatever you are trying to achieve, whatever goal you've set yourself, never lose sight of it. All of us can get so caught up in the immediate moment that we can lose sight of what our ultimate goal is.

- How many times in your life have random events had a negative impact on you? How have you reacted to them? Did you feel overwhelmed? It's a very understandable reaction. Were you able to adjust to the circumstances and find a way to keep moving forward? I think that's the key to resilience. It's finding a way to keep moving forward towards your goal no matter what the circumstances, no matter the obstacles, no matter the pain.

- Has there been anything you were working towards that you gave up on? I want you to think about why you gave up, and if there is anything you would do differently now? Do you feel inspired to try again? So much of life is failure. The most important part is to not let failure have the final word. Try, try and try again. It is the only way to succeed.

The Dark Place

What is the dark place? For me, it's where all the pain is. I've been to visit it many, many times in my life. When I'm way down in that hole, the pain cuts through all my crap and forces me to look deep within myself. Am I willing to suffer? Am I willing to keep pushing forward despite the agony?

Every time, the pain offers me a deal. It says to me, 'If you stop, Ed, I stop too.' That's the temptation on offer. But if I end my suffering, I end my dream. That's the biggest question the pain asks when I am in the dark place: Can I endure the suffering in the short term, or will I quit and be forced to live with losing forever?

I tell myself, there is nothing I *can't* endure. There is no moment I *won't* endure if it means achieving my dreams. I tell pain to back right off. I suffer now and live forever as a winner.

The first time I heard someone describe the dark place in the way that I'd experienced it was the great Muhammad Ali. There's a man who knew a thing or two about pain and suffering. There's a quote from him that I have framed on the wall in my gym. It says, 'Suffer now and live the rest of your life as a Champion.' Ali realized that you needed to suffer for your happiness. Ali knew that if he was going to become a Champion with a capital C, he'd have to endure all kinds of pain and suffering to do so.

Ali told a story to illustrate how far he was willing to push himself. If Ali and his rivals were to have a competition, where they swam out into the ocean and kept swimming until only one of them was left, Ali believed he would be the winner. Ali believed he would outlast Joe Frazier, George Foreman, Sonny Liston, Henry Cooper, Floyd Patterson, heavyweight legends all. He was convinced he would be the only one willing to suffer through the cold, through the fear, through the pain and still be willing to continue further into the darkness. The rest would all quit before him.

The point of the story was to show Ali's mindset. Once he climbed through the ropes, he was prepared to take his opponents to the darkest of places and keep going. He bested them, dominated them, knocked them out or forced them to quit. I took no end of inspiration from Ali's story.

I've always taken losing very personally. My competitiveness is a big part of why I'm so obsessive. It's both my gift and my curse. I have a drive to win that pushes me to my absolute limit. The blinkers come down and all my focus goes on doing whatever it takes to achieve my goal. Without doubt, my obsessiveness comes at a cost to myself and the people around me. I know how much I personally suffer because of my drive to be the best. I see how it affects my relationships with the people that I love. Do I wish I could switch it off sometimes? That's a hard question to answer. My competitiveness and my obsessiveness have made me ruthless. Ruthless with myself most of all. No shortcuts, no skipping sessions, no easy days.

They say hard work beats talent when talent doesn't work hard. You only have to look at Thor to see the genetic talent at his disposal. The guy is a freak. He stands 6ft 9in and last time I noticed he weighed in around 24½ stone. For the fight, there wasn't much between us in weight, but his height gave him a definite advantage. That was an important detail because in boxing the taller fighter has what's known as 'reach' on the other boxer. Simply put, it meant Thor was able to reach me with a punch when I couldn't reach him from the same distance. I had to try and close the gap, and the only way to do so was to step into danger if I wanted to be in range to hit him. Lindon and I had cooked up a little plan to counteract Thor's advantage long before the fight.

One part of that plan was to take Thor to a very dark place in the ring, to take him to a zone where he wanted to quit sitting on his stool rather than come back for another round in the ring with me. How did I to do that? When I knocked him down in the second round I inflicted pain on Thor. Pain like he had never experienced in his life.

I brought Thor into a deep, dark place during our fight. I made him feel fear, pain and loneliness. As you know by now, I wasn't able to completely deliver on my plan, and I make no excuses for that; so credit to Thor for pushing through against the pain I inflicted on him.

You might have figured out by now that the dark place exists in the mind. It is the mind's reaction to pain. The pain is asking a binary question: quit or stick? As an athlete, I know the fight is always to convince my mind to keep pushing, to push through the pain and make it irrelevant to what I am trying to achieve. In many ways I'm very comfortable with pain, both physical and mental. I feel like I've lived in the dark place for large parts of my life. The physical pain I've always been able to accommodate. But the mental pain has taken me a longer time to reach a balance with.

My struggles with depression are very well documented. I don't mind telling you about it. I've been dealing with it for more than fifteen years now, and I know only too well the pain it causes. Depression is a dark place that you go to, and it brings with it a dark pain. In a very bleak way, depression is just another pain that asks your mind the same old question – are you going to stick, or are you going to quit? It's a sneaky one. It steals the joy from your life, and it makes every single day a struggle. It is a pain that has caused me no end of torture down the years. It's something I've had to learn to live with as I believe my depression will never be cured. Medication and psychiatrists have never worked for me; instead I've had to develop my own set of tools and strategies to manage it.

My first experience with depression happened in my mid-teens when my nan got sick. I had to grow up very fast when the extent of her diagnosis became clear. There was no way to cushion the blow – she was going to die from this illness and there was nothing anyone could do to change that. At that age, I thought everyone was invincible, and I didn't really understand things like illness and death until I saw it happening to someone I loved.

My nan was diagnosed with leukaemia, which is a type of blood cancer. It decimated her and seeing a woman who was so kind and full of love deteriorate was devastating for me and for all the family. I felt like I was losing the only person who really understood me. She was the one person who I could speak to about anything that I was going through, and she would listen without a word of judgement. She was pure love, and my anchor in so many ways. Her diagnosis meant that I had to face up to the reality that she wasn't going to be around for very much longer. But I wasn't ready to confront my sadness and anxiety or make my peace with the fact my nan was dying.

Instead, I went off the rails in reaction to her diagnosis and I stayed off the rails for quite a few years. I was in my late teens and already feeling pretty lost at that time in my life, and my nan's diagnosis just compounded that sense of meaninglessness in my life. I told you already that I was once a serious prospect to represent Great Britain in swimming at the Olympics. I loved the sport, but I had a problem with the people around it who were in charge, the elite level coaches and administrators. I found them negative and authoritarian. I engineered a way to get myself thrown out of a programme, The World Class Potential Programme, which was an established pathway to the Olympics. It wasn't too long after that I got expelled from school, too. It seemed that I was intent on destroying anything positive or constructive in my life.

I think, in a strange way, I created these problems as a distraction. They were a way for me to put my head in the sand and not have to face the hard truth. My nan was dying and there was nothing I could do about it. These are big overwhelming emotions to wrestle with, even at the best of times. When you factor in that I was really still a kid and struggling to figure out what I was going to do with my life, it's probably not much of a surprise that I went looking for things that would distract me and leave me numb. I found two things that were very distracting, and very numbing – drinking and fighting.

For the next few years, I spent plenty of time doing both. Looking back, I can see that I was struggling with depression. I wasn't taking responsibility for the pain it was inflicting on me and the people who loved me. I found it much easier to get blackout drunk on whisky or smack someone in the face than deal with my serious mental pain. I wanted to do something great with my life. I wanted to make my nan proud. I wanted to make my family proud. But I couldn't see a way to do that. The distance between where I was in my life and where I wanted to go felt massive.

It's fair to say I fell into a really dark, deep, horrible hole. I had horrible thoughts about myself, that I was worthless and that I had no future. It was when I had thoughts of killing myself that I knew I needed to get help. Looking back now, I'd say I should have asked for help so much sooner. I should never have let it get to a point where I was having suicidal thoughts. I needed to acknowledge that I was suffering with depression. I saw doctors and I was put on Prozac. I know both of those supports have been amazing for people suffering with depression, but for me, it didn't feel like they helped.

It got to the point where I was really struggling to get out of bed in the morning. And it was during this time that I discovered the gym. Hallelujah! It was an absolute revelation to me. I felt like I had discovered my calling in life. Lifting heavy metal was just the thing to lift me out of the dark place I found myself in. Going to the gym made me feel better because, for the first time in what felt like forever, I had purpose. The structure of a training routine and having clear goals to work to – that changed my life. I think it is no understatement to say it probably saved my life too. It was the gym that helped me pull out of that dark hole and gave me the focus that I needed in my life. It helped me see a way out of the dark hole I found myself in and it offered me the chance to change the trajectory of my life. Pretty soon a vision formed for what my life could be.

I initially wanted to be a bodybuilder like my hero Arnold Schwarzenegger. The more time I spent in the gym, the more it became apparent that my true talent was lifting very heavy weights. Gradually my focus shifted from bodybuilding to Strongman. I knew in my heart I could win World's Strongest Man, even though that dream seemed so big, so impossible. I broke my dream down into goals, and those goals became my obsession and my salvation. It's a strange thing to say, that an obsession saved me, but it did.

It was around this time that my nan's final days came. She had endured her illness with supreme grace, and she had accepted that her journey was almost at an end. I am forever grateful that I was there with her, holding her hand as she passed. My biggest fear, the trigger for so much anxiety and depression, had happened – my nan was gone, and I'd never see her alive again. I also knew she was at peace, and all of the pain and suffering she had endured was over. I'd have given anything for my nan to live but if that wasn't to be, I'd be much happier for her to be at peace than in any kind of pain. I made my own peace with her passing in that way. Before she slipped away, I made a promise to her that one day I would win the World's Strongest Man. It became my quest in life. My purpose was to fulfil the promise I'd made to my nan on her deathbed, and I became obsessed with fulfilling it.

One thing I've learned about myself is that there is a part of me that needs purpose, that needs obsession, in order not to fall back into that deep, dark hole. I don't understand why that works for me; I just know that it's my way of keeping the depression in check. For me – and I stress this is just for me – it's better than speaking with professionals or taking anti-depressants. The combination of having a big purpose and endorphins seems to keep me on an even playing field by and large. It's why I had continued to work out so much even after I had conquered my dream and fulfilled my pledge to my nan. It's a reason why I was so keen to accept the fight with Thor. It was the first time since 2017 that I have been consumed by something in the same way that I was consumed by winning World's Strongest Man. It felt peaceful, in a strange way, to be so focused and dedicated to one goal.

All that being said, I still go through periods where depression takes hold. I have a lot of demons and I reckon I'll be struggling with them for the rest of my life. The one really positive thing is that I feel much better equipped to recognize and manage my depression these days. One of my big tells that things are getting on top of me is when I go very quiet. If depression is starting to kick in, I go into my shell and I try to avoid people, even those closest to me, even Alex, because I don't like talking about how I feel. Again, I'm not saying that's the best way to manage it, I'm just being honest about how I am when I'm depressed.

Definitely one of the worst things about my depression is that I lose sight of who is important to me in my life. I feel disconnected from my wife and from my kids. It feels horrible whenever I'm in that dark place again. I get really snappy with people and I feel the anger burning in me. That's when I know I need to pummel myself in the gym to release the stress. It's the only thing that re-centres me and pulls me out of my funk. I'll do a serious boxing session or a proper heavy weights session and that releases the tension for me. For whatever reason that helps me to clear my mind and pulls me out of my own head for a moment.

It's weird. I can have my family around me, I can feel pretty happy with where my life is, I can feel satisfied with what I have achieved, and yet I can still feel lonely. Why do I feel lonely? Why do I feel sad? Why does working out help? I wish I could tell you; I wish I could figure it out. But I can't. All I can do is deal with it.

I've talked about my experiences with depression in the hope that it removes some of the shame or stigma associated with it. The single best thing I did when I was struggling with my mental health was to speak to those people closest to me about what I was going through. By naming the problem and sharing it with the people I trusted, it helped me to feel less alone and more supported.

As you well know by now, for over ten years my obsession was to win World's Strongest Man. The all-consuming commitment to that quest was what filled the void for me. I believe it was an obsession that saved me in many ways, but there was a dark side to the pursuit as well. I was working as a truck mechanic in 2015 while battling to make my dream come true. During this period,

I felt like I didn't really have control of my life. I was working for someone else in a job that I didn't enjoy when all I wanted to do was turn pro as a Strongman. The frustration with my life, coupled with the failure to capture the deadlift world record due to a disqualification, resulted in a pretty severe bout of depression. I was signed off work for nearly six months. As hard as that period was, it provided me with the time and the financial support to allow me to turn professional. By July 2015 I was able to fully commit all my time and my energy to becoming World's Strongest Man.

Over the period from turning professional in 2015 until I won the title in 2017, I put on 32 kilos or about 5 stone in body weight. By the time I eventually captured the title I was pushing the scale at 196 kilos which is just over 31 stone. If you look at pictures of me from that era, I was bloody humongous. The reason I was that heavy was very simple – to lift heavy you've got to be heavy. I knew I was pushing my body to its absolute limit, but the size was a means to an end – winning World's Strongest Man.

However, we live in a world where people feel like they

can comment on how you look, especially on platforms like Instagram and Facebook. The path I chose to achieve the goal I set myself attracted a serious amount of negativity. I'd get comments like, '*He might be World's Strongest Man but he's as fat as butter.*' Or they'd say, '*I wouldn't want to look like that no matter how much money you gave me.*'

Those comments hurt. People were tapping out comments on their phone without a thought given to how those words impacted the person on the receiving end of them – me. It wasn't nice for me to read those comments at the time. It wasn't nice for me to feel like I was a target that people could throw darts at. But I learned how to deal with it. Nowadays, I choose to use any comments like that as motivation to stick it to the people who feel like they are entitled to talk bad about me. Anybody who feels like they can put me down should know that I'm fuelled by their comments. I turn that negativity into something I can use as motivation.

Over the years as I went through my career as an athlete, the obsession with getting bigger and stronger took a toll on my physical health and my mental health. I went to the gym to get away from my demons, but sometimes they followed me through the door. Physically, it's not natural, and it certainly isn't healthy to walk around at over 30 stone. I say that as someone who's been there and done it. My liver and kidneys were always right on the edge of failing, my heart was under massive stress and my skeleton was groaning under the amount of weight it was being asked to carry. Why was I putting my physical health into such a precarious position? Because I had an 'all or nothing' mentality driving my physical transformation. I had convinced myself that I was either going to win World's Strongest Man or die trying. I was undeterred by the physical limitations of my body. Getting bigger, it was not just about size for size's sake. The bigger I was, the more I could lift. But the bigger I became, the closer I edged my body to the abyss of a total shutdown. I was reckless. I recognize that now but at the time I simply didn't care. I did not care if I died trying to win WSM and given the size I was, 'win or die trying' was a live possibility. I really could've died.

Doctors kept a very close eye on my physical health as I grew bigger and bigger. There were regular check-ups, ECGs, heart angiograms, blood tests, all of which were intended to monitor my health and keep on top of anything untoward happening. My kidney and liver markers were always right on the brink of going into shutdown. Whenever the numbers got too close to the threshold, the doctors would tell me to scale it back. But even then, I wouldn't listen to them and I'd keep pushing it. I knew I was gambling with my life but at the same time I felt my life would only be worth something if I could win that title. The conundrum at the heart of my obsession – I could only win it if I was willing to risk everything.

One doctor said to me, 'If I were to draw up a list of people in the UK right now who are most at risk of heart attack, most at risk of stroke, I would put you, Edward Hall, top of both those lists by a country mile.' It was scary to hear that from a doctor and those words haunted me every night before bed. Sleep terrified me. Every time I closed my eyes, I was convinced that I wouldn't wake up. To live under the shadow of that was tough in the extreme. Yet there was a part of me that was able to put that anxiety to one side. Each morning that I awoke, I continued on my path to getting bigger, undeterred and undaunted. The fear of death was the price

I was willing to accept in order to achieve my dream. That's why it felt like I was skirting the line of suicide because I was willingly and recklessly taking these risks with my body. But I didn't care. I needed that trophy home on my mantelpiece.

Five weeks before World's Strongest Man, I was at home in bed on a Saturday night and something wasn't right. My heart was racing and I couldn't get it to slow down. I got up and went to the kitchen, I put on my heart-rate monitor and it bleeped at me that my heart was doing 140 beats per minute. To put that into context, that's about the rate it gets up to when I'm running at a fair old pace. I tried to stay calm and I told myself it would peter out in a bit. I sat down, flicked on the TV and waited for it to settle. The monitor then bleeped at me again – my heart rate had plummeted to 60 beats per minute, and I got really dizzy. At this point I was very scared and I thought I was in real trouble with my heart. The doctor's warning about my risk of stroke and heart attack were on repeat in my head at this point. I called to Alex and asked her to send for an ambulance.

The ambulance paramedics arrived and they hooked me

up to an ECG. They told me my potassium levels were through the roof and it was causing my heart to spasm. I had increased my potassium intake on the advice of doctors as tests had shown my levels were very low. I had been taking potassium tablets, eating bananas and drinking coconut water to compensate and, in the process, I overdid it and poisoned myself. I refused to go to hospital because I didn't want it to become a newspaper headline: 'Eddie Hall has a heart attack'. You can imagine what the reaction on social media would have been to that.

The paramedics told me to sit and relax, drink loads of water and that would flush it out. I sat watching the TV for six hours while I drank litres and litres of water then slept it off. Even all that wasn't enough to scare me into taking the doctor's orders seriously, reduce my bulk and give my overstressed body some much needed respite.

I had come too far and I was too close to turn back. I needed to see it through. I knew all along I was gambling with my health. I promised the doctors that after I won, I would follow their instructions to the letter. I'd reduce my size and I'd stop trying to push my body beyond what it was physically capable of. I was lucky. My gamble paid off, I won the title, and I did so without major long-term damage to my health.

But what would I have done if I hadn't won in 2017? I think you can guess my answer. I would have kept going. I would have remained in that limbo of going to sleep each night not knowing if I would wake up the next morning. That aspect was so mentally tiring, and physically, I would have just kept getting bigger and bigger, putting even more strain on my already overburdened system. There's every chance I would have pushed my body beyond the limit of what it could withstand resulting in a heart attack, stroke or even death.

Thankfully I was able to lay my obsession to rest with the win in 2017, but I do reflect from time to time on the very dark place I brought myself to in order to achieve the win. I still struggle to reconcile how I could have placed myself in such jeopardy, how I could have risked my wife becoming a widow and my children being left without their father. Those were the stakes throughout 2017. But the thing is, I was doing it for them; I was risking it all for a better life for them. Was losing my life worth the gamble? I'm still here and breathing with the win in the bank, so I can say yes it was worth it. But what if the roll of the dice hadn't gone my way? What if I had gone to sleep and never woken up?

More recently, 2020 and 2021 have been very difficult years and it's taken a lot of people to the darkest of places, me included. For me, it all started with a little tickly cough. I remember I was in a training session with Pat, and Hannah (Team Beast's videographer) was there filming, and every few minutes my tickly cough kicked in. But I didn't think anything of it and I finished out the session no problems. The next day I was in a boxing session and I started sweating profusely. Lindon, my coach, asked if I was all right and I told him I was all good. I carried on and had a cracking session. Then I woke up the day after that boxing session and I felt like death. At this point the alarms bells were ringing. I knew Pat and I needed to go and get a Covid test, because we had been in very close quarters with each other. We did the Covid test and both of us tested negative. I thought to myself that was a bit weird given the symptoms. We went back again the next day, did another test and tested negative again. Neither of us felt great but we had tested negative for Covid. We hadn't trained in a few days, and we were wondering if we should get back into the gym. We decided to go for a power walk just to see how we fared. We got back and both of us were broken. I couldn't speak after it. I had no energy and I crawled straight into bed. I woke up the next morning and that's when I knew something was seriously wrong. I was so drained of energy, I couldn't keep my eyes open and then the fever started. I did another test and finally tested positive for Covid; it took a few days for the infection to register a positive result.

Pat and I decided to have some time off training. We knew for certain it was Covid and we decided to rest up, let the virus take its course and then crack on once we were both better. I felt all right then, mentally and physically, to be honest. I knew I had the virus, and I knew it was just a case of taking things steady and resting up.

But I didn't improve, and instead I went downhill. On day nine, after the positive test, the fever took over. I had a constant temperature, always 40 degrees or over, from the second I woke up to the second I went to bed. The fever was so bad that I couldn't sleep. I had bags under my eyes and they were horrendous – I looked like I'd come back from the dead. I was at death's door literally. I went upstairs to the bathroom and I coughed out this massive lump of blood into the sink. I looked at this lump of blood, took a massive huff of breath and said to myself, 'I'm going to die.' I thought that was the takeover point, when my lungs had been taken over by this virus. My whole body sank and I thought to myself, 'This is my time.'

I spent my birthday sitting on the couch crippled by the fever which was getting up to 42 degrees. Alex and I did a bit of googling and learned that any fever over 41 degrees is when your brain starts to boil, so clearly I was in very dangerous territory. I then became unresponsive, so Alex rang for an ambulance and they came out and got me into the hospital. The doctors put me on a drip and gave me some Covid medication. By the evening, I was feeling well enough to go home but by no means cured.

During this period, I had every single symptom that Covid listed. The diarrhoea, the coughing up blood, the fevers, everything. It was horrendous. The fever was the worst of it. I was constantly either too hot or too cold. It was brutal. It was nearly a month after my first positive test when I started to pick up a little bit. I thought I was out of the woods. I got back training and I realized I had long Covid. My lungs were shot. I did two rounds of boxing and I was absolutely gassed. I was almost falling unconscious in between the rounds because I was oxygen-deprived. It took me another six weeks to get back to any sort of fitness where I could actually do exercise for more than say three or four minutes. And then, just as I was really starting to feel better, I got Covid again.

I went through the whole process all over again, but the second time wasn't as bad. I had another ten days of fever. I developed a swollen lymph node on the side of my neck about the size of a tennis ball. I can tell you that was super painful and infected. Between the two bouts of Covid and the recovery periods, I reckon I didn't train properly for five months. I was just an absolute zombie during that time. I couldn't sleep or eat properly. I'm not used to having that sort of feeling of helplessness, of not being able to get up and do something for myself. I found it impossible to sit and do nothing but rest. I couldn't do it. I lost 18 kilos in body weight, going down from 160 kilos to 142 kilos. I felt helpless. It destroyed me mentally more than physically. I just went into this really bad depression for those months. As soon as I was able to, I got myself into the gym and got moving. Even if it was just one or two rounds of boxing, it helped me so much mentally. It took me months to build up on that. It was a solid five months before I was fully fit. Lindon knows my fitness better than anyone, and I can remember the session where he said to me, 'You're back.' It was like flicking a switch; my fitness and strength just sprung back all of a sudden.

I had a long battle with Covid. It was an awful experience and I wouldn't wish it upon anyone. I can't say I'm glad I've had it, because I'm not. My illness made me realize how serious it was. I thank my lucky stars that I came out the other side of it because a lot of people didn't.

There have also been a lot of mental health issues associated with the pandemic. I have lost a number of friends to suicide during this period. It's a tragedy and it breaks my heart, not only for the friends I've lost but also for all the people left behind who love them.

One of my best friends had been suffering with depression for a long time and in 2020 he took his own life. He hanged himself on Facebook Live. I know that's a shocking thing to say but I want you to be shocked. The decision to die by suicide is shocking. The first question everyone asks when they hear of a suicide is why did they do it? Depression is not something you can rationalize. It takes you to the darkest of places and it overwhelms you with negativity. You lose sight of who you are and you lose sight of the fact that many people love you and need you. When you're in that frame of mind and thinking of ending your life, what you need most is someone in your corner.

I know my friend was active on social media not long before he died. I do think social media played a part in him deciding to take his life. I'm not going to go on a rant against Facebook or Instagram or any of the rest of them. Social media is a tool that amplifies a message. If you put it out there on social media that you're feeling depressed, people, by and large, take the mickey out of you. If you're depressed and you reach out for support on there, you're most likely just getting more negativity directed back at you. Negativity is just going to send you further into the darkness. It has to. My friend needed positivity in that moment. Every time I think of my friend, who had so much going for him, I also think of all the people who loved and needed him. He had a business; he had a girlfriend and kids. All of that was gone in an instant.

Before he killed himself, he was brought to a mental hospital to be assessed because he was having suicidal thoughts. Do you know how long he was kept in for? An hour. Then he went and killed himself. The mental health system in this country is not fit for purpose. There is literally no funding going into it. I feel for the people who work within that system, the nurses and doctors, who are saints. They are getting no support, no money, nobody to fight on their behalf.

What if I found myself in that position? What if I went to a hospital asking for help and I didn't get the help I needed? What then? It scares me because I know if my friend did it, I could do it. I could lose sight of the love in my life; I could lose sight of how important it is to keep on living.

I'll be the first to say, I struggle to talk about my feelings when I am in a dark place. I think it's something men in general struggle with. It's scary to open up about what I'm feeling as it makes me feel vulnerable. But it is so important to do it. At the same time, it's crucial that if someone does open up about their depression that it is met with kindness and compassion.

I have been honest about my struggles with depression so that, in some small way, it might help someone else to open up to a friend or seek help if they are feeling depressed. To anyone reading this, I urge you in the strongest possible terms, if you are feeling depressed or suicidal, talk to a friend or talk to your doctor. Talk to someone because you can't suffer in silence. There is no glory in trying to overcome something like depression by yourself. It's the darkest of dark places, but there is always a way back to the light.

I spoke with Paddy McGuinness about his experiences with depression. Paddy is such an open and generous soul. He was very forthcoming in our conversation. Paddy said, 'Sometimes with depression, it's happening but you're not aware of it. It's not like a sprained muscle that you know immediately is injured. It's the people around you who notice usually that you're not yourself. For me, it was my wife who said to me I should see someone because my behaviour wasn't doing me any good. I wasn't biting people's heads off, she just noticed that I wasn't myself. I had sessions with a few therapists before I met the right one for me. The best thing I ever did was seeing someone; I mean that sincerely.'

Depression can affect anyone and we all find different ways of dealing with it. I found a way to manage my depression through going to the gym. For Paddy, he found a way of dealing with his depression by speaking to someone. I think the most important thing to remember is that no matter how horrendous things might seem, there's always something or someone out there who can help.

Key Learnings

- The dark place exists in your mind. It is a reaction to pain. The question the pain is asking your mind is, are you going to quit or are you going to push through? Have you ever been to the dark place when you've been trying to achieve something? It might be trying to squeeze out a personal best running time or breaking a max lift in the gym. It could be trying to change careers or following a dream. The dark place is a gift because it confronts you with an extreme test of your abilities and it teaches you so much about yourself. Whatever it uncovers in you will surprise you. My hope is that when you find yourself there, you will discover that you are stronger, more resilient and tougher than you thought you were.

- My competitiveness is a big part of why I'm so obsessive with my training and preparation. It's both my gift and my curse. I have a drive to win that pushes me to my absolute limit. What drives you? If you can tap into that, it will provide you with an almost limitless source of motivation.

- My competitiveness and my obsessiveness have made me ruthless. Ruthless with myself most of all. No shortcuts, no skipping any sessions, no easy days. Are you ruthless with yourself? Do you sometimes deviate from your plan? Anyone who has ever achieved anything has a ruthless, selfish streak within them. Find yours!

- I have been honest about my struggles with depression so that, in some small way, it might help someone else to open up to a friend or seek professional help if they are feeling depressed. There is absolutely no shame in being honest about your mental health. It is not a sign of weakness but a show of the greatest strength possible.

The Smelling Salts

It took me months and months of training before my boxing game finally came together for me. It felt really satisfying for all of the elements that I had been working on with Lindon to come together – footwork, head movement, feints, blocking, counterpunching – all of these skills that I had been drilling for thousands of hours in the gym. I learned first-hand how technically demanding boxing is. You just have to keep working and working at it.

Lindon, who has spent nearly forty years in boxing, would say himself that even he's still learning. That's boxing. It is a sport that demands commitment and graft but you'll never master it. I love that. As well as my satisfaction at the development of my skills, I really started to feel my fitness improve. I had shed 35 kilos or 5½ stone, and I was feeling very svelte at the 160-kilo mark. I don't think I had been 25 stone since I was 25! I felt so confident in my sparring sessions, my hard work was paying off and I was feeling super positive.

All of these were very good things. In fact, they were great things. I was at the exact moment in my journey where my hard work, and the hard work of all the team around me, was paying off. It felt fantastic and deeply satisfying. I had made so many sacrifices to get to this point. I remembered all of the days where I had failed miserably to put into action Lindon's instructions; but when my boxing game finally started to click, it was the best feeling in the world. However, it was also a very dangerous thing.

It's a fair question to ask, how is improvement a dangerous thing? One word. Complacency. It was at this point in my journey that I had to be at my most vigilant against complacency. It was such an easy trap to fall into, especially when I felt like I was making such good progress. The temptation was to take my foot off the pedal a little bit without realizing it. That's complacency at its most dangerous, when it's so subtle that you can't even feel it creeping in.

What is complacency? It's a complicated thing which can have many causes and can show up in many different ways. I've encountered a few different types of complacency over the course of my career. The most common type of complacency is what I like to call the smug git. I call it the smug git because it's the kind of complacency that comes from being far too pleased with yourself. I've seen it many times in my competitors and might have even fallen victim to it myself in the past. The danger with falling into the trap of being a smug git is that you're so pleased with yourself and the work you've done so far, that it leaves you underestimating the dangers you face and blinds you to your deficiencies. Without a doubt, it's this kind of complacency that stops you getting the best out of yourself. If you're satisfied thinking that you're pretty good, you're never going to become great.

The most common cause of the smug git is improvement. Take me and my boxing journey. I started with zero boxing skills. I improved thanks to the incredible mentoring by Lindon, the support of Pat, and of course my own hard work. When it all started paying off, that's exactly the moment the self-satisfaction kicked in. It's human nature to feel satisfaction from improvement. I got a buzz out of how I developed, especially compared to where I was at the beginning of my journey.

Was I happy with my progress? Yes. Had I reached a point where I was satisfied with where I was at? Absolutely not. That was the tension in the tightrope I was walking. I needed to recognize the improvement I was making to see that the training was working, but I had to keep striving to get better and better. How did I do that?

I'm going to share with you a few of the tools I used to keep me focused and stop me from becoming a smug git. I think of them as being like smelling salts for my mind. These tools helped me guard against complacency as well as refocus and re-energize my efforts when my motivation was flagging.

Whenever I felt even a hint of complacency, the first thing I did was have an honesty session with myself. I asked myself, 'Am I still as hungry to improve as when I first began?' It's human nature to ease off the throttle as you improve, and there were definitely days where my hunger and motivation weren't at 100 per cent. On those days, I used my visualization techniques to remind me of the dangers I faced. The thought of being knocked out on pay per view in front of millions of people was a brilliant way to crush any complacency and light a rocket up my backside to get back to work. Fear is a great motivator. Never underestimate its power. By visualizing a negative outcome, it planted a seed of fear that motivated me to push myself to continue to improve.

The other great tool I used to combat complacency was to measure my progress against my goals. There is nothing like a hard dose of reality to evaporate any complacent thoughts or behaviours. You might recall in Chapter 2 I talked about preparation and goal setting. No matter the challenge, I always look at the goals I've set myself and I compare them with my progress to date. How am I doing? Do I need to reassess my goals to aim higher? Or are there areas that I need to give attention to because I'm not where I want to be? Goals that are measurable give me something definitive to work towards. For example, for the fight it was one thing for me to say I wanted to drop weight. It was another to say I wanted to weigh in at 160 kilos the night before the fight. Even better than that was saying I needed to drop 2 kilos every two weeks if I was going to weigh 160 kilos on fight night, and stepping on the scales every fortnight to see how I was doing. Assessing my progress against very well-defined goals is always a brilliant way to blow up any complacency that might be seeping into my mindset.

For the fight, I was so lucky to have a really strong team of people around me. Being accountable to them was another tool I used to guard against any decline in my performance. If I didn't show up for a physio session, if I missed a boxing session or I skipped a recovery session then I was letting myself down, and I was letting down the people who were working their backsides off so that I could get better. Missing sessions, or even showing up and only putting in a half-hearted effort, would be unprofessional and disrespectful to the people I worked with. How would I have reacted if Pat skipped out on a session or if Lindon was only half interested when we were working the pads? I'd tear them a new one. Of course, there were days when I didn't want to have my muscles scraped by the physio, or I didn't want to do ten three-minute rounds of sparring or I didn't want to spend an hour in my hyperbaric chamber. Those were the days when it was especially important to show up and do what needed to be done. I always gave my all and I got through it. That's what it means to be a professional. I show up and I do the job even when I don't want to.

There is another type of complacency which is rooted in the process. None of us like change, especially if it is a departure from a way of doing things that has delivered results. We become prisoners of our own success. But in order to get better we have to evolve our approach. Let me give you an example to help explain. It took me five years to qualify for World's Strongest Man. It took me another two years to make it past the qualification round. Finally, it was another four years of competing before I eventually won the bloody thing in 2017. It took me ten years in total from when I competed in my first novice strongman event until I became world champion.

Do you think my training regime, my diet and my recovery remained the exact same all the way through my journey? Of course it didn't. I had to experiment with everything in order to improve. I didn't even do training for the events when I first started, and I was still winning competitions. I might have had enough raw talent to win regional comps, but there's no way I would have won national or international competitions on talent alone.

In order to continue to progress in Strongman, I had to evolve my approach. That meant changing up my training, and even if I had a short-term dip in results, I was willing to do it to achieve my dream of winning World's Strongest Man. For a long time I never did stretching and recovery sessions; now recovery sessions are a central part of my programme. I looked at my rivals, people like Brian Shaw, and questioned how he approached his Strongman training to learn from him. Why wouldn't I? He was without doubt, consistently, a winner on the circuit, so clearly there were lessons to be learned and incorporated from his process. I pushed my own evolution too. I experimented with my training methods, with my approach to recovery, even with my mindset. I don't think there was anyone in the Strongman world thinking about building a house of gains when I was doing it. But if you want to win you have to evolve. It's not survival of the fit, it's survival of the fittest.

It's easy to fall into the trap of being a prisoner to the methods that bring success. You do what you've always done because what you've always done has always worked. Until it doesn't. It can be a tricky thing to get your head around because it seems counter-intuitive. Surely if your methods have brought you success, then those same methods will continue to bring you success? Wrong. In sport, in business, in life, people are always searching for an edge. If you want to stay relevant, if you want to stay in contention for the medals, then you have to keep improving, innovating and pushing the boundaries. If I had kept to the same training methods when I first started in Strongman, even though they were bringing me success, I would have eventually stagnated, and the other competitors would have passed me by.

The best way to guard against process complacency is to be curious and to be brave. Can you imagine if I only used some version of the same workout routine since I first started in the gym? I would've stagnated and hit a plateau in my improvement long ago. The body needs to be constantly challenged to grow and so does the mind. I'm always switching up my routine, and I'm so lucky to have Lindon and Pat to help. I've learned down the years; the change of routine challenges my body and makes me feel refreshed and re-energized. A change sometimes is as good as a rest.

There's a big difference between *thinking* you're better than everybody else and *knowing* you're better than everybody else. I first learned that lesson back in 2011. I went into England's Strongest Man really complacent about the field of competitors I was up against. I was convinced I was going to win it without even breaking sweat. In my mind, all I had to do was show up and collect the trophy. I was that confident of the win, that after each event, instead of prepping for the next one, I'd have a lie down and grab a bit of sleep. All the other competitors were doing their stretching, getting themselves mentally psyched up for the next event, while I was in a corner snoring my head off. It's actually pretty mortifying as I think back on it. I wouldn't dream of behaving like that if I was in a competition now.

I completed the last event and what do you think happened? I had drawn with a guy called Ben Kelsey, who is a strongman from Scotland and a very impressive competitor. No disrespect to Ben, but I did not expect to find myself drawing with him at the end of the competition. I expected to have destroyed the field and I expected to be sitting on top of the table with a record haul of points. There was a yawning gap between my expectations and reality. I had been complacent about the athletes I was competing against, to the point of arrogance, and now I was paying for it.

When there is a draw in Strongman events, the rules state that the winner will be decided by countback. That means the judges count back over the events and whoever has the most first places across the various events is declared the winner. So, we did that and guess what? Still tied. Ken and I both had the same number of first places. In order to separate us, we had to do a sudden-death event. The judges decided it would be a Farmer's Hold, which involved us both holding a weight in each arm until one of us couldn't hold them any more. First to drop was the loser.

Ben and I set ourselves, made sure our hands were comfortable and in the right place for the grip, then we picked up the weights and the clock started. We were standing facing each other so that it became as much a mental test as it was a physical test.

I can still remember us staring at each other; I tried to front like I could do this all day even though with about a minute gone I could feel my grip starting to slip. At this point my complacency is long gone over the hills, and I think – Ben is going to beat me. How did that happen?

I had one final card to play. I looked at Ken and I said, 'What are you doing? You're not going to beat me even if we stand like this for the next two days. Just drop the weights and end the pain for yourself.' We were both in that dark place of pain I spoke about, and I watched as those words crumpled poor old Ben. He dropped the weight a few seconds later. That showdown showed me how much of the battle is in your own head – both in terms of pain and complacency. There must have already been a little bit of doubt in Ben's mind and my words just gave that doubt the weight it needed to tip him into quitting. But there is no question, I put myself into a position where I almost lost and the reason for that was because of my complacency towards my competitors.

I'm not too big to say there was quite a bit of my own ego and arrogance fuelling my behaviour. I believed I was better than anyone else there, and I was, but not by as much as I thought. In fact, just by thinking that I was better than everyone else, I very nearly wasn't. It was a complacency born of over-confidence. After that competition, I had to think about it, think about how the smug git had almost cost me the win, and adjust my behaviour so that it wouldn't happen again.

I took that lesson on board. I never underestimate my opponents. Now I always assume I'm going up against the ultimate boss who has trained hard and wants to win just as badly as I do. There is a part of me that believes I worked twice as hard as Thor in training. There's also a part of me that respected the danger Thor posed. Both beliefs have a place in my mindset and the shift in mindset is everything. Instead of thinking I have enough in the tank to beat all comers, I think I need to bust out these last few reps because that's exactly what my opponent is doing. I need to train better than him if I am to be better than him.

It is a little bit of fear infusing my mindset, a fear that I won't wring every drop from my potential, or that I could possibly lose. The fear drives me to train the hardest I can, to prepare the best I can, and ultimately to perform to the limit of my abilities. That's all I can ask of myself – to perform the very best I can. I know if I can do that, I will be there or thereabouts on competition day.

I think that story illustrates very well how my own complacency towards my rivals almost came back to bite me in the backside. It was a complacency rooted in overconfidence and a belief that I was so much better than my fellow contenders. That kind of thinking is dangerous on a couple of levels. It encouraged me to underestimate my rivals on competition day, which is completely the wrong mindset to have. Since then, I view every opponent as the supreme threat, and I prepare and perform according to that belief.

Where competitor complacency is really dangerous is in the subtle but massive impact it has on your mindset. Never forget, it is mindset that dictates how you approach any challenge or competition. If I underestimate my rivals, it will seep into my mindset and diminish my work ethic.

It starts by sacking off the last few reps in a set. But pretty soon it's skipping out on training sessions all together. That's a recipe for epic failure.

One final thought on competitor complacency. It might be true that I am better than my competition, but if I'm only measuring myself against them, then it means I'm always aiming to do just enough to beat them. In other words, it is my competitors that are setting my standards when it should be *me* setting my standards. If I had set my standards according to other people, I'd never have realized my potential.

Why do power athletes use smelling salts in the first place? I, like every other power athlete, use them because it gives my body an immediate adrenaline rush. It's similar to the fight or flight response we spoke about in the first chapter. The bang from the smelling salts kicks your whole system into gear, giving your body the juice to perform at the absolute optimum.

I think it's fair to ask why I need a shortcut to access peak performance. I'm not superhuman, and like everyone else, I have off days. I have days where it's a real slog just to even get through a session. On those days, the smelling salts act as a jump-start to my system, increasing my sharpness and getting me into gear. As useful as the smelling salts are, it's important to have mental tools to support me as well.

I've spoken to you about the various mental tools I use which are like smelling salts for my mind. They help me to guard against the various complacency traps which I have fallen into in the past. They also help me to do something which sounds boring but is imperative to progress – maintain consistency.

Why is consistency so important? If I show up every day to put in the work required to get better, then guess what? I get better. That's what consistency is. It's showing up every day and putting in the work when the work is hard. I've got to go to my absolute limit every session and leave nothing left in the tank. It's hard to empty myself in every training session and it requires a real capacity to suffer. But guess what? That's what separates me from everyone else.

It's through hard work that I learn, and it's through working hard every day that I improve. Improvement is the little present that you get when you have the grit to get through the grind every day. Being consistent in my training, in my diet and in my recovery has been the difference between failure and success for me. Consistency requires superhuman levels of hard work and an unswerving commitment to achieving a goal. There is nothing magical or mysterious about what I am telling you. The things done every day lead to great achievements over time. Who knew?

The best athletes in the world can perform at a consistently high level day in and day out, week in and week out for months and even years on end. They can do that because they are focused, committed and consistent. They can deliver a performance on competition day because they are always hovering in and around that level in training. It's the other major benefit of consistency. They reach a level where they're able to deliver a performance almost at will.

You can get into this state where it doesn't matter how hard the thing is, you can do it with your eyes closed. This is called the flow state – the holy grail of performance.

I experienced it in World's Strongest Man 2017. All through the finals, which take place over two weeks remember, in every event I competed in I was either winning or finishing in the top three. After each event I walked off and I wasn't out of breath, I didn't even feel fatigued from the exertion. I looked at the other competitors and they were rolling around gasping for air. I didn't get why everyone else was gassed because I felt phenomenal. I was in the zone. I was in the flow state. I will never, ever forget it. I mean, I pulled a deadlift of 472 kilos on a really extra-long stiff bar and it was ridiculous. I lifted it like it was nothing – it was as easy as picking up a kitten. I got stronger as the competition went on which I still think is crazy. I competed in thirteen events; it was two weeks of completely battering my body day in, day out and yet I had never felt so strong. I remember thinking to myself, 'I'm 31 stone and I could literally punch my way through a brick wall.' I felt so in control of my body at that size. It was freaky. There's no man on the planet that I was scared of. I was invincible. I felt like the Terminator. I was definitely in my flow state and I felt amazing.

I loved competing in World's Strongest Man 2017, and not just because I won it. It was the performance I was most proud of across all my career – a signature performance. I was able to perform at the level I did because I implemented all the concepts I've talked about in this chapter. There was zero complacency in any form. I didn't underestimate a single one of the competitors. To be honest, I was so focused on myself and my own performance that I didn't even have time to think about anyone else. There was no smug git thinking in my mindset; I'd been working for ten years to win the World's Strongest title and I'd still not done it. The obsession to win only burned all the stronger after my injury in the 2016 edition scuppered my chances. There was no complacency in my preparation. I'd spent the entire two years as a professional strongman searching for any edge I could find.

My training regime was perfect. I had an army of specialists – physios, sports psychologists, doctors, hypnotists. You name it, I had it. I even built my own hyperbaric chamber just to squeeze an extra 1 per cent from my recovery sessions. Finally, I was consistent. I did the hard work. I didn't miss one training session, I didn't miss one meal and I didn't miss one minute of any recovery session. In short, I was perfect, and I was perfect for two years.

I had to be. For all that work and sacrifice I was rewarded with a perfect two-week performance at World's Strongest Man 2017.

Lindon Newbon

I think that what I've learned from Eddie, really, to be fair, is that unless you've got 100 per cent commitment as an athlete, you're not going to be elite. I've had lads in the past who've not quite met that level. From Eddie I've seen what makes an elite athlete. Ed's got an extra little bit. I've learned that is what it takes to be elite. It takes that extra little bit and it's something in his make-up. That's Eddie Hall.

For the fight, it was the same. Consistent work, day in day out. Leaving no stone unturned. Recovery, diet, boxing skills, ringcraft. I was up against a competitor who, when all's said and done, was pretty bloody impressive. One big punch from him was enough to knock out any old smug git. But me, I did not go into the fight with a smug attitude. I went into every session like a beginner – willing to learn, willing to do what I was told and willing to give it everything.

Complacency is such a sneaky git. It can creep in at exactly the moment when you're flying high and on track to achieve your goals. I asked James Haskell about his experience with complacency in his career. James said, 'Complacency wasn't a big issue for me in my career. If ever I thought I was cutting corners, the voice in my head would call me out. This was far stronger than any desire to sack off some core work at the end of a gym session.'

I really identify with what James says about the little voice in his head pulling him up if he ever went to cut corners in the gym. I have the same experience and I think it relates to my preparation. If I have a plan that I'm accountable to, then there's no way in the world I'll skip out on a session. Not happening. Ever.

I told James about my own brush with complacency competing in England's Strongest Man 2011. James' observation was, 'When you're standing still someone else is moving forward.' It's a very important lesson to take on board and use as a guard against complacency. Be consistent in doing whatever it is you need to do to achieve your goal. Putting in the hard work every day when the work is hard. Because if you don't do it, you're standing still and someone else will be passing you by.

Key Learnings

- The most common type of complacency is what I like to call the smug git. I call it the smug git because it's the kind of complacency that comes from being far too pleased with yourself. The danger with falling into the trap of being a smug git is that you're so pleased with yourself and the work you've done so far, that it leaves you underestimating the dangers you face and blinds you to your deficiencies. Without a doubt, it's this kind of complacency that stops you getting the best out of yourself. If you're satisfied thinking that you're pretty good, you're never going to become great.

- Measure your progress against your goals. There is nothing like a hard dose of reality to evaporate any complacent thoughts or behaviours. Always look at the goals you've set yourself, and compare them with your progress to date. Ask yourself questions like, 'How am I doing?' 'Do I need to reassess my goals to aim higher?' 'Or are there areas that I need to give attention to because I'm not where I want to be?' Goals that are measurable give you something definitive to work towards.

- There is another type of complacency which is rooted in the process. It's easy to fall into the trap of being a prisoner to the methods that bring success. You do what you've always done because what you've always done has always worked. Until it doesn't. In sport, in business, in life, people are always searching for an edge. If you want to stay relevant, if you want to stay in contention for the medals, then you have to keep improving, innovating and pushing the boundaries.

- There's a trap I call competitor complacency. There's a big difference between *thinking* you're better than everybody else and *knowing* you're better than everybody else. Competitor complacency encourages you to underestimate your rivals on competition day, which is completely the wrong mindset to have. View every opponent as the supreme threat; prepare and perform according to that belief.

- Consistency requires superhuman levels of hard work and an unswerving commitment to achieving a goal. The things done every day lead to great achievements over time.

ROUND 8

The Good and the Greatest

You might remember in the last chapter I said there's a big difference between *thinking* you're better than everybody else and *knowing* you're better than everybody else. Over the course of my boxing journey, one question nagged me: 'What separates the good from the greatest?'

It was 2011 when I was rocking up to Strongman competitions thinking I was better than everybody else, and yet I was barely squeaking out any victories. It took me another six years until I was able to prove to myself, and the world, that, beyond doubt, I was the alpha.

What did I learn over those six years that kept me on a trajectory to the top? What did I actually do that made me into a world champion? How did I go from good to great?

I'm obsessed by this question. As you already know, I started this journey with zero boxing skills. Under the tutelage of Lindon, and with the help of Pat, I developed my skills far faster than even I thought possible. As we got into the final months before the fight, everyone in Team Beast felt the intensity increase. The final preparations ratcheted up the intensity and pressure to another level.

I'd been preparing for this fight for nearly two years, thanks to Covid and injuries. I felt like a kid at Christmas knowing that the endgame was in sight. The final camp was masterminded by Lindon. He's been there, done that and bought the T-shirt a thousand times over. It was all about sparring and sharpening me up so that I peaked on fight night.

The key thing was that we timed the final stages of training for the fight. I did loads of sparring, which allowed me to polish my boxing skills and sharpen my ring fitness. I lived like a Spartan for those final few months, and I loved it. I felt my mindset really focus and there was a sharp edge to my sessions as I faced the final test. The mountain was now coming into view.

In the downtime between sessions, I thought a lot about how little time there was left until the fight. After so much time together, Team Beast had fewer than a hundred sessions left. We were in the endgame of this journey, but we knew we had the opportunity to go and do something special together. As much as my team were literally in my corner, I knew it was me who had to get in the ring. Every moment counted in those last couple of months. It was crucial that I wrung every drop out of myself. Which is why I was so obsessed with the answers behind the question, 'What separates the good from the greatest?'

Look at the icons in sports – Muhammad Ali, Michael Jordan, Tiger Woods, Serena Williams, Diego Maradona, Usain Bolt – why do those names burn so much brighter than those of their rivals? Was it because of their talent? Was it genetics that separated them from the rest? Or did they possess some kind of freaky skills? Was it because they had an X factor or whatever you want to call it? Those athletes are all once-in-a-lifetime talents. I'm fascinated by their journey to the very top. All of them, even from an early age, seemed like they had the seed in them to do something special. But, you know what? So do loads of people. Why did these athletes become such superstars?

I thought of my own experiences as well, and what I had learned along the way. Even if I do say so myself, I've come a long way. Maybe from some people, not very much was expected of me. But I've smashed world records, won the title of World's Strongest Man, been a TV presenter and done all sorts besides. How was I able to achieve those things?

Let's start with the obvious – genetics. I'm a good 6ft 3in, and that means I'm bigger than the average bloke in the street. Then again, if you are comparing me to the biggest beasts of Strongmen, the Brian Shaws, or the Thors of this world, I'm coming up on the smaller side. A height advantage in Strongman helps on a couple of fronts. The taller a strongman is, then the bigger the frame is to hang muscles and bulk on. Remember you have to be heavy to lift heavy things. Also, taller strongmen have longer levers for pushing, pulling and lifting which makes a big difference, especially when the margins at elite level are so small. I don't have the height or the levers of all those freaks that are closer to 7ft tall. But, the one thing I have in my back pocket is something called the Hercules gene, which is about as good as it sounds. It's quite a rare thing to have but dead handy when you're a strongman.

Our bodies are a genius piece of kit. The things they can do, and the way that they do them, is extraordinary. They have some very complex systems which make sure everything is running smoothly. One of these processes is to limit the amount of muscle mass we can add to our frames. Our body produces a hormone called myostatin which prevents the production of muscle fibres and also prevents existing muscle fibres from getting too big. Essentially, it is a muscle regulator for the body. But I have a mutant X-men gene which causes my body to produce a much lower level of myostatin than regular people. The result? My body's muscle limits are much higher than everybody else's and I can hold muscle mass a lot easier as well. It partly explains why, even though I was significantly smaller than Shaw and Thor, I was able to pretty much match them in weight give or take a kilo or two. What I lacked in height I was able to compensate for in bulk and brute force.

Genes are all well and good, but there's also another element to factor in – I had to show up in the gym and do the heavy lifting. Sure, my body contained some special gene that allows me to push beyond the limits of other people. But if I'd sat around on my backside for a decade rather than putting in the work, I wouldn't be where I am today. Good genetics are a nice bonus to have in your back pocket, but without the hard work they're useless.

What do I mean when I say, 'hard work'? We've all heard people bang on about hard work, but what does it actually involve in real life? See, I've always believed that I could achieve great things, as long as I was willing to work my backside off and give it my best. That might seem like an oversimplification relative to my achievements, but looking back over everything, it all boils down to having a work ethic. I've always had one way back before Strongman. I think back to growing up as a kid and how I gave everything to swimming. I cycled miles before dawn to do a session in the pool. Or even to my time when I was working as a truck mechanic, running a doorman business and training for Strongman. To keep those three plates spinning required a ferocious appetite for hard work. And I tell you what, I've got an appetite on me. Here's the thing – I actually *like* working hard. I'm not someone content to sit around all day and wait for something to happen.

I love a challenge. I never have and never will back down from one. I love them because they put me under pressure and force me to deliver. One thing that has shone through so clear to me, and everyone around me, was just how much I enjoyed preparing for the fight. It was amazing to have something to dedicate myself to entirely, especially with everything that had been going on in the world. I really would have struggled if I hadn't had something to consume so much of my thoughts and energy during Covid. I don't know how much of my love for challenges is down to nature or nurture, so I'll say this – I'm good at nurturing my nature.

One of the things in my nature is to be competitive. From growing up with my brothers, to swimming, to Strongman and now boxing, I've always thrived whenever there's been competition. I've nurtured my competitive drive so that it's useful to me, rather than getting me into fights on the streets or trying to drink more pints than somebody else on a night out. These days, my competitive nature lights a fire in me, in a way that I can't really describe. It's my competitiveness that makes me obsessed with winning.

Loving a challenge, my competitive nature and being obsessed with winning have all played a major role in my development as an athlete and as a person. I've always been passionate about whatever I've done with my life. From swimming to Strongman to boxing, it's never felt like a chore to train or to compete.

Of course, there were hard days where I felt tired or stiff and sore, but I never thought – God, I wish I was anywhere but in the gym. Even when I felt flat, I've always been able to push through and get it done. I know that if you can't get it done when you don't want to, you won't be able to do it when you do – like on competition day. As you might have clocked by now, I like winning. The idea of sacking off a session never crosses my mind. If you want to win, you've got to commit to the sessions. Simple as.

The other major factors in sculpting my mindset have been adversity and failure. I've never been one to allow a setback to define me. In fact, as you've already read in Chapter 5, I've always tried to use failure as a signpost directing me to future success. I've always found a way to move forward whatever obstacle I've faced or failure I've encountered. The thing I've learned from all those experiences is that resilience and perseverance are what define you, not failure.

What made me resilient? That's almost as difficult to answer as what separates the good from the greatest. There's a load of things, but I think it boils down to something Ross Edgley said. I'm very willing to suffer for my happiness. I've always viewed any adversity as an opportunity to grow rather than an obstacle to my progress. I'm never happier than when I'm being pushed right to my limits and tested to the point of failure. Otherwise, what's the point in taking on a challenge? Even if I fail, I'm still learning.

Of course, I don't enjoy failing but I've learned to value it. Why did I fail? Being able to answer that question without getting defensive is the key. If I can answer that question with hard-nosed honesty, then I am halfway home. Most of the time the truth is that every failure has the secret to future success. It can be a painful process; I pick over every mistake and figure out all the ways that I was wrong. It's not pretty. But when I've been tough enough to go through that process, all the lessons to learn are there. All the things I've got to work on are right there. The rest of it, the perseverance if you like, is just grinding on those lessons, putting what I've learned into practice.

I've always brought a forensic and scientific eye to my improvement. I've always thought deeply about my training, my diet and my recovery. I know those three elements all have to work together for me to make gains. I've spoken to you already in Chapter 2 about my philosophy of building a house of gains from individual elements. In my journey to win World's Strongest Man, I searched for anything that could give me an edge within each of those three elements. I've evolved because I've been willing to take a risk and put what I've believed into practice. I've done that all the way through my journey from lifting weights in a shed in Stoke to figuring out how to pull half a tonne off the floor. I've broken through into terrain that was unmapped, and everybody else believed was unreachable.

There is another lesson in that. I've kept laser focused on myself. I've always set my own standards and I've always strived to get better every day. I think those three words boil down the essence of my mindset, very simply – better every day. I was never overly concerned with what the big beasts of Strongman were doing because I couldn't control that. I never focused on the fact that they were taller and heavier than me. All I had in my control was what I could do. For that reason, I always benchmarked myself against myself. From day one, that was a game I could win. Was I performing better than the last time? If not, why not? These sound like pretty simple tweaks, but it took me time to incorporate them into my mindset. They're bloody hard to do all the time, day in, day out, week in, week out. Whenever I felt like my focus was slipping, I'd make a conscious decision to pull it back. Everyone else was irrelevant. The only thing that mattered was me, and what I was doing. That was it.

No matter how much success I had, or what I achieved, I never dwelled too long in the afterglow. Pretty quickly I've moved on from victories and achievements and the question has always been what's next? Where is the next challenge? What is my next goal? I've never been satisfied, I guess. I'm not saying I'm not proud of what I've done, or grateful for the opportunities I've had. But there's always been a hunger in me to keep learning, to keep growing. The only way I can do that is to keep challenging myself and keep setting myself goals. What's the next chapter? What's the next thing? It's the journey, this circle of accepting challenges and setting goals; then immersing myself in the hard work and sacrifice required to eventually achieve what I've set out to do.

Lindon Newbon

It's the extra mental attitude and the elite way of thinking. Eddie won't be denied. He will push through. If we say we do twelve rounds, Eddie will only walk away after doing twelve rounds. Eddie has an ability to push through, to ignore the body's pain. He's very good at that.

As you know by now, I've never been shy about telling the world what I'm going to do and then going out and doing it. I've been doing that since I was five years old. There is a reason 'Back Up Your Bull' has become a calling card for me. I do what I say I'm going to do, even when everyone else says it is impossible. I believe doing that plays a large part in building a legend and burnishing a legacy. Why do people still love Muhammad Ali? He was the greatest because he said what he was going to do before a fight, and then he went and delivered on his words in the ring. That to me is amazing. The self-confidence and belief he demonstrated was outrageous. At the time, his critics called him arrogant, but he convinced himself and, more importantly, he convinced his opponents that he was the greatest.

I've incorporated some of that approach into my mindset because it forces me to be better. I love the pressure it puts me under to have to deliver on what I've said I'll do. It's a way of backing myself into a corner and it forces me to come out fighting. It's also an element that helps to keep me accountable and committed to my goals.

There's a mental advantage to be gained over my

competitors by saying what I want to achieve and taking that on, on my own terms. By going out saying I was going to win World's Strongest Man or that I was going to pull half a tonne, it knocked my competitors out of their focus on themselves, and it forced them to think about me. I was living rent free in their heads every day of that competition.

Going into World's Strongest Man 2017 I thought Brian Shaw was my biggest competition for first place. It is pretty funny looking back at how relaxed I was throughout that whole competition, given what was at stake. Talking myself into believing I'd already won gave me an edge over my opponents. It was part of my game plan. By announcing I'd already won it, it actually took the pressure off me and placed it on all the other competitors. It toppled their focus – they should have been thinking about their own preparation, visualizing their own performance in the various events. Instead, they were thinking about that so-and-so Eddie Hall, standing in first place on the podium. They were visualizing their own failure! What a gift!

I did see Brian Shaw as the biggest obstacle to my

winning that year. Brian was already a legend in Strongman, as well as being a great ally and friend to me. Throughout the competition, Brian and I were very tight; we hung out every single day. I'd hired a truck and every evening Brian and I would go to a steakhouse we'd found up the road from the hotel. We'd rock up and smash through a mountain of steak, and we'd get the carbs in with baked potatoes and chips and whatever else. Two big units chowing down after a day of competition under the hot Botswana sun. We were fierce competitors with each other in events, but once we were outside of it, we'd have a laugh and chew the fat over how the day had gone for us both. Those are pretty good memories looking back and we supported each other through the two weeks of the competition.

The night before the final, we followed the same routine of going to our steakhouse and loading up on the carbs, but neither of us said a word about the showdown the next day. We ate in silence, hopped in the truck and it was only a quick spin back to the hotel. We were both in the lift taking us back to our rooms. I remember looking at the sign in the lift that said do not exceed 500kg and doing a quick tot in my head. I figured between me, Brian and my physio who was with us, we've got maybe 10 kilos to spare. The doors opened on my floor and me and the physio stepped out. Then I turned around and I looked Brian square in the eye, and I said, 'Brian, good luck tomorrow, mate.' Before the doors of the lift shut, I backhanded him in his privates. Brian's jaw dropped to the floor and before he could say or do anything the doors shut. I looked at my physio and said, 'That's his sleep ruined tonight.'

I tell that story with my tongue in my cheek. I don't think me whacking Brian in his bits was the difference between me beating him or not. But I do know this. Every single competitor in World's Strongest Man that year thought of me as a threat. They knew I was a threat because of the body of work I'd put together in the two years leading up to it. I talked up the big bad monster that was already living in their head – doubt. I acted like I had already beaten them because I knew that would feed their doubt and it would irritate and distract them. As well as that, acting like I'd already won freed up my energy to just focus on myself, be a professional and get the job done.

I know from my own experience, the mental side is so important because when you reach an elite level the margins are so fine. From a physical perspective, there's very little to separate the top four or five athletes in Strongman, or any other sport you want to choose. What separated me from the rest in 2017? My mentality. All of the tools in my mindset formed the armour I wore into that competition. The competition was a culmination of all the hours of training, all the sacrifices made, all the failures and lessons learned. It was only during that competition that the hunger to get better was briefly silenced. At World's Strongest Man 2017 I found the answer to my question – was I good or was I the greatest? That year, I was the greatest.

So, coming back to boxing, what I needed to remember going into this fight was that amongst those who have succeeded at the very highest levels, genetics and talent are only one small part of the story. What counted for so much more was attitude and work rate. I couldn't do much about genetics at this point, but attitude and work rate were completely in my control.

As I geared up for the home straight, I told myself,

'Never underestimate the power of passion.' One thing I've learned about myself is that I need to love whatever it is I'm doing – even when I hate it. I need to have that same thing that I found in the gym all those years ago. Thankfully, I had that love for the sport of boxing. For me, that was more than half the battle. That meant that no matter what, I wanted to get better every day.

Hard work is a massive part of achieving any goal, and it was firmly within my control how hard I worked to achieve my goal of beating Thor. You know me, I'm no slacker. Loving a challenge, loving the training and preparing for that challenge, and a healthy enjoyment of competitive rivalry all contributed to me putting my nose firmly to the grindstone.

This is one of the things I reckon people miss – if you truly are consumed by what you are trying to achieve, then the hard work stops feeling like hard work to an extent. It isn't a grind, it's a reason to get out of bed in the morning. Every hour in the gym, every mile on the road, it's a step towards something bigger.

This chapter is all about what separates the good from the greatest. We've covered a lot of aspects – genetics, an appetite for a challenge, a healthy competitive streak, an ability to learn from failure and resilience in the face of adversity. Most of these things I've listed are encompassed by mindset. Paddy McGuinness said, 'Most people have it in them to do something, but actually the hardest part is mentally pushing yourself to do it.'

Paddy is highlighting just how important mindset is if you're going to achieve anything. Mindset is grit, determination and resolve. It's all in your head and it's all in your control. You decide what your mindset is. That's a powerful message that Paddy highlights.

I spoke to Ross Edgley about taking on a challenge and wanting to be the best at something. Ross said, 'The athlete in me just wants to do something that completely rips up the rule book. Swimming around Great Britain, people were like, why don't you swim across the English Channel? I was like, it's been done. I've no interest in doing it at all. When I find something that I can uniquely do, and someone says that's stupid, that's when I'm like, right, hold my beer.'

The thing that really resonated with me is how Ross said he wanted to do something that completely ripped up the rule book. I know what that feels like. Everyone said I couldn't do the 500-kilo deadlift and I completely demolished people's preconceptions of what is possible. I think the lesson is, whatever you're doing in your life, make it epic. Rip up the rule book, don't listen to anybody who says it's impossible and instead go out there and prove them wrong.

Key Learnings

- There are many factors that separate the good from the greatest. One factor that is completely non-negotiable is showing up and putting in the hard work. I've always believed that I could achieve great things, as long as I was willing to work my backside off and give it my best. Having a work ethic can take you a long way towards achieving your goals. Resilience and perseverance are what define you, not failure. Be willing to suffer for your happiness.

- Nurture your nature. I love a challenge. I never have and never will back down from one. I love them because they put me under pressure and force me to deliver. It's in my nature to love a challenge and I nurture my nature by seeking out challenges that will test me. Similarly, I'm very competitive. I've always thrived whenever there's been competition. I've nurtured my competitive drive so that it's useful to me. It's my competitiveness that makes me obsessed with winning.

- Resilience and perseverance are what define you, not failure. I'm never happier than when I'm being pushed right to my limits and tested to the point of failure. Otherwise, what's the point in taking on a challenge? Even if I fail, I'm still learning.

- How do you respond to difficulties, obstacles or failures? Do you allow them to overwhelm you or do you come up with a plan to keep moving forward? People talk about resilience like it's something mystical. It really isn't. Shift your mindset into a place where you welcome adversity as something to test yourself against; if you can view failure as an opportunity to learn then you'll begin to build resilience. You need resilience if you are going to achieve your goal. Resilience is the mental toughness required to execute a plan that keeps you moving forward towards your goal.

ROUND 9

The Taper

The great Muhammad Ali once said, 'It isn't the mountains ahead to climb that wear you out; it's the pebble in your shoe.' I've talked about Ali a lot in this book, and there's good reason for it. He knew what he was on about. Thor had been a pebble in my shoe for a number of years. I looked forward to finally being done with him once and for all, so that I could get on with all those other mountains that were ahead of me.

As I completed my final training camp and I was right on the cusp of finishing this journey, I reflected back on all of the work I had put in. I couldn't help but think about how far I had come. The first few months, where so much focus was on dropping weight, redefining my body shape and learning the fundamentals of boxing, were possibly the hardest months of training. I had really come to appreciate that a sport like boxing demands 100 per cent commitment and dedication. I had to build my house of gains from the floorboards up. Boxing is a massively technical sport, and Lindon had been my mentor and guide, drilling me so that the movements had become second nature. I knew that in the ring with Thor, I wouldn't have time to think. When he threw a shot at me, I needed the muscle memory to kick in and pick the right option.

I loved the interest this fight with Thor generated. I had been documenting my journey on my YouTube channel. All through my preparations there had been this din of chatter about what training I should have been doing, when I should have been sparring, who I should have been sparring with. All of it nonsense talk from the keyboard warriors who thought they knew better. I chose Lindon as my boxing coach because when I first met him I recognized that we were cut from the same cloth – meticulous, driven and clinical. I put my trust in him and he repaid that a hundredfold. I was very raw when we started working together. Just have a look at the YouTube videos of our early sessions! Lindon led my training because he understood how to build a boxer. He knew that there was no point in throwing me into a ring early on to spar, practising bad technique and getting schooled by a pro. What would that have done for my confidence? We had to build up my skills and develop my ringcraft to a point where I was ready. We had to time my sparring with my run-in to the fight, otherwise I would leave my best work behind me in the gym.

Lindon Newbon

You've got to have times where you ease off because, at the end of the day, he is The Beast but he is still a human being. Eddie will push and push and push. Part of my job is to get a boxer or an athlete peaking at the right time. It's no use being on fire in the gym, and then on fight night being tired and lethargic. It means you've left your best work in the gym. It's peaks and troughs with fitness. You will come to your peak and that should be when we fight. Then you'll ease off because your body can't sustain that peak forever. Part of my job is to get Eddie coming towards the peak. What we'll do is, four or five days before the fight, we'll do nothing. It's just rest up time. It's about filling the muscles full of glycogen and getting your energy stores back. The biggest problem with someone like Eddie is that he won't want four or five days off before he boxes. He'll want to be training but he won't be, he will be resting. There will be no negotiation; he will have to listen.

The taper – the ten days before any physical contest or competition where I have to wind back all of my training and let my body recover. I can tell you as a professional athlete, I love and hate this part of the process in equal measure. I love it because the end is in sight, all of the hard work has been put in the bank and I'm ready to draw on it come competition day. I hate it because I enter a state that feels like purgatory.

I put my body through hell preparing for this fight, and with the taper I had to completely switch gears into recovery mode. I found it so hard to do that, to sit and do nothing. I was used to the daily grind of training; I was used to putting in the hard work required in order to deliver a performance. All that stopped and was replaced by lots of sitting around and waiting. That's why it felt like purgatory. It continued to feel like purgatory for me until I got in the ring and did business with Thor. Every single day I had to remind myself that it was about being a professional and doing what had to be done. This was the time to relax, this was the time to fuel up with carbs, relax all of the muscles and just let everything chill.

Even though I found this transition into doing nothing really tough, as always, I had the experience of World's Strongest Man to draw on. I remember the taper for that. Ten days out from my 2017 win, I stopped all training, which just felt absolutely bizarre. I was so close to the moment of truth with this obsession that I'd been chasing for two years. I had to stop my training routine, not touch a weight, do no lifting whatsoever. My days were filled with stretching, some hot and cold treatments, some physio and drinking lots of fluids. Serious point, there's nothing worse than dehydration. Drink your fluids, stay hydrated. It took all my strength to not go back into the gym. I felt like I was squandering these precious few days before the competition. Was I going to get stronger with ten more days of training? Not bloody likely. Also, a year prior I had planned and plotted all my sessions all the way up to World's Strongest Man. I hadn't missed one of those sessions. I'd been absolutely perfect.

As I did my taper, I gave myself a slap to remind myself that this was all part of the plan – come competition day I was primed to fire. All my little niggles and injuries had time to settle down and recover. My muscles filled with glycogen. My sleep and foods were on point. And of course, my hydration levels were Aquaman perfect.

The plan delivered for me, because not only did I win World's Strongest Man, but I put in a personal performance of a lifetime. I felt myself getting stronger and improving as I went through the competition rounds. Actually, I felt unstoppable as I progressed through the competition. All that just reinforced my self-belief and confidence. I never had any doubt about bringing home the winner's trophy from Botswana.

I adopted the same approach for the fight. It was chill time. I let the muscles heal and be primed to perform come the showdown. I had done all of my sessions, I hadn't missed one and I'd been training like a beast. I knew that I was not going to get any faster or any better as a boxer. It was about being professional, resting up and being ready to bang on fight night.

One of the great opportunities of this purgatory time was that it provided me with the mental space to really sharpen and focus my mindset. In the last chapter I told you that it's mentality which separates the good from the greatest. In the exact same way that I allowed my body to rest, recharge and reinvigorate itself for the fight, I used this same taper period for sharpening my mentality. It was a golden opportunity to resolve any mental doubts or performance anxiety that might have been lingering in my mind.

I went through an inventory of all the tools in my locker. I had the chance to pull them out, take a good hard look and make sure that everything was in perfect working order. It gave me comfort and confidence to know there were no lingering doubts, that my mindset was on point and I was ready to rumble.

So how did I do it? Well, first up I reflected on why I

had taken on this challenge to fight Thor, what my goals were when I started and how close I was to the finish line. As I approached the final threshold, the base camp before climbing the mountain if you like, I was thinking a lot about all of the work that I'd put in to get to this point. I was thinking about Team Beast and everything they had put in to help me. I was thinking about Alex and the kids and the rest of my family. I was not trying to get myself psyched to the point where I had adrenaline coursing through my system for ten days. That would be a recipe for no sleep and a terrible performance. I suppose I reminded myself of what I'd suffered through and who I'd suffered for.

A big part of this was to make sure I had my finger on the trigger of my fight instinct and that it was ready to rock when I needed it. As you know, it is my superpower and 100 per cent I needed it in the ring with me. To test the trigger, I thought of the reasons why I had agreed to the fight in the first place. I thought of how Thor disrespected me and my victory after World's Strongest Man. I thought of how he had continued to speak about me, calling me a cheat and the general scorn he had shown towards me. I thought about my son Max and my daughter Layla. I thought about Alex. I thought about how I wanted to make them proud, and how I wanted to right a wrong. Even thinking about it made the hairs on my neck bristle and the blood flow faster in my veins. Everything was as it should be.

You might think this is where my mind was in the locker room in the moments before my ring walk but you're wrong. There was so much adrenaline coursing through my body at that point but I was trying to be professional and stay focused on the job at hand. In those final moments, I tried to get myself in the best possible place to deliver the performance and be clinical.

One common stress during the taper is performance anxiety. I understand it. If I've worked my guts out for something, then I want to deliver when it matters. Otherwise, what's the point of all the preparation? It's here where mentality really separates the best from the rest.

Performance anxiety is something I encountered quite a bit in the early part of my career, especially building up to the big events like UK, Europe and World's Strongest Man. It took a while for me to figure how to best manage it. My brain is so obsessive, and I usually distract and silence it by pouring all of myself into training. When I'm in a training block where I have a very heavy workload, I'm usually so knackered by the end of the evening that I can barely keep my eyes open, let alone worry about my performance. So, moving into a period where I can't train, a period where I have to sit and do nothing at all, you can imagine how I can get. My mind wants to skip ahead to the competition day, and it wants to obsess about how I am going to perform. How do I pull my mind back to the present moment and stop my thoughts from worrying about how I'm going to perform on comp day?

For me, the key to silencing the anxiety was in my preparation. Especially in my early years competing in the Strongman competitions, I always had this nagging feeling that I hadn't done enough work in advance of the events. That makes it sound like I was skipping out on a training session or whatever. I wasn't. But I knew in my bones that I could prepare better. I could train better. I could eat better. I could recover better. But I was hamstrung by two little things which I didn't have enough of – time and money.

Once I got myself into a position where I had free rein to train when and how I wanted; when I could afford to ramp up my diet; and I could do the physio and recovery sessions that I'd longed to do. Then, and only then, did I begin to feel like I was preparing to the very best of my ability. The performance anxiety before competitions disappeared. Why do you think that was?

It's because I knew I couldn't have done any more training; I couldn't have eaten any better and I couldn't have recovered any better. My preparation was done to my standards, in the way that I wanted, and I executed to the very best of my ability. There were no lingering doubts or worries about missing a leg session or not doing an evening in the hyperbaric chamber. Everything was on point and carried out to the very best that I believed possible. The preparation became the cure.

Even now I still have the odd moment of anxiety around a performance but crucially I know how to knock it on the head. I remind myself that I've put everything I can into my preparation, and I have absolutely nothing to worry about. I know come D-Day I'll be ready to bang, I'll be ready to back up my bull, whatever the challenge.

During this purgatory period, instead of burning my energy with anxiety, I build up my confidence and I know I'm ready to deliver.

One of the tools I used day in and day out during this period was visualization. I am a hyper-visual person, and this tool has been, and continues to be, a key weapon in my arsenal. I've participated in big-time events in the strongman arena but this thing with Thor was on a whole other level. It was a different beast to World's Strongest Man or breaking world records. Thor and I, mano-a-mano with a ton of pride on the line, were taking part in something that neither of us had ever experienced before. It had all the elements – fighting with a pay-per-view audience across the world, and a proper nasty rivalry. How did I prepare for a professional boxing match with all of the trimmings?

It was impossible to replicate exactly what I was on the cusp of, but visualizing it was most certainly a big help to me. In my mind's eye I saw the dressing room in the hours before the fight. Lindon and Pat were there to work me through my warm-up and get me physically prepped. There was a clinical atmosphere in our dressing room.

I was there to do business, to be a professional and to be ruthless in the ring. There was no shouting and screaming or punching of walls. I was managing my energy and staying focused on delivering my potential.

My hands were wrapped by Lindon and someone from Thor's team was observing. You might wonder why someone from Thor's team was in my visualization watching me getting my hands wrapped. In boxing, someone from an opponent's camp always watches the hand wrapping to safeguard against any cheating. Less honourable boxers than me have, in the past, tampered with their gloves to give them an unfair advantage. Then it was gloves on and into the bear pit.

I've performed in front of big crowds in the past, and I drew on that experience to visualize the ring walk. It's a funny one because in the past I've always drawn energy from the crowd. If you look at the video of the world record deadlift in Leeds, you can see I'm loving the noise the crowd are directing at me. For this fight visualization, I stayed very focused on the job at hand. I saw myself deep in my zone as I walked to the ring, keeping my heart rate nice and steady before that bell rings.

During these days of the taper, I went through that visualization exercise multiple times. Lindon has been such an asset in this regard because he's been there and done it so many times. We planned every moment of the day of the fight. I knew when I was warming up, when I was stretching, when I was eating, and when I was making my way to the dressing room. All that might seem like overkill, but it goes back to what I was saying about preparation and planning being the best way to deal with anxiety. If I knew what I was doing and when I was doing it, then I could just focus on the job I needed to do. Having my plan in place allowed me to visualize how the day would go. It might sound mundane to think through every moment, but it was preparation for the final test. There were no surprises or last-minute hitches, and the visualization exercises added another level of insurance that the team and I had thought everything through.

If I ever had trouble getting my mind into a place of visualizing positive outcomes, I would go back to my preparation. I'd think of a time I slipped a punch in sparring or when I connected with a straight right. Then I'd think about connecting that straight right to Thor's head. Visualization helped me to prepare by anticipating what was to come. Visualization helped me tap into a very powerful and positive energy that drove me towards my goal. More than that, it built my confidence and self-belief as I stood at the foot of the mountain I was about to climb.

I did think about the mountain in front of me during this time and what I had to do to conquer it. I knew what it took to win World's Strongest Man. I'd been around Strongman for ten years and I'd been professional for two years before I won it. In many ways, I already knew what it took to win it before I finally brought home the trophy. But the fight with Thor was my first time entering the ring and participating in what was essentially a professional boxing match. I knew I had done my work physically, but I needed to interrogate my mindset to ensure I was happy to go to the dark place I spoke to you about in Chapter 6.

I mentally prepared myself for the fight to be brutal. I knew that meant pain – both inflicting it and accepting it. I was not going to slip every punch. I was going to get caught with jabs. I learned from my sparring that it's an intense thing to be in the ring with someone else. Everything else faded away. It was just me and my opponent locked into each other's stare, responding only to the feint of a shoulder or the flicked-out jab searching for connection.

The dark place is a key part of my mentality. During the taper, I made sure that I was ready to go there. I needed to know I was steeled for entering that crucible of pain once the bell rang and the fight started. This is the boxing game. It's big time, the stakes are life and death and nothing less. I couldn't have any weakness or doubt in my mind when I entered the ring. I needed to be prepared to do what I had to do.

Every challenge has a moment of truth – a moment that decides the outcome. The taper is the best time to prepare for it. I knew only too well, no matter how much training, preparation and visualization I did, I couldn't anticipate the moment of truth. During the taper, all I could do was ensure I was physically and mentally right on the edge and ready to bang. I was there; without doubt I was there. I knew when I was in the ring and the pain asked the question of me, I was ready to answer it.

This chapter is all about dealing with tapering off from training and having yourself in tip-top mental shape before the main event. I spoke to James Haskell about how he dealt with nerves the night before a big game. James said, 'Before games for England I would watch highlights reels of myself play or maybe Richie McCaw or other guys that I really wanted to aspire to be, and that's how I would derive confidence.'

I think what is really interesting is that James used visualization too when he was feeling the nerves the night before a game. He looked at YouTube videos of himself making runs and breaking tackles. Or he looked at others in his position who he aspired to be like and watched them play.

I think that's a big lesson you can take from this chapter and apply. When you find yourself the night before your moment of truth, remember all the work you've put in to get to this point and take confidence from that.

Key Learnings

- The taper – no matter what the goal is you've set yourself or challenge you've taken on, you'll reach this point in your journey too. It's important to recognize it because it is a transitional point – the journey is almost complete, and the final test lies just over the horizon. I can tell you as a professional athlete, I love and hate this part of the process in equal measure. I love it because the end is in sight; all the hard work has been put in the bank and I'm ready to draw on it come competition day. I hate it because I enter a state that feels like purgatory.

- What are the triggers you use to get your central nervous system booted up so that you can access your fight instinct? It's crucial to ensure that it's ready to fire when you need it. Ahead of any challenge I urge you to reflect on your journey to this point. Think on the reasons you took on a challenge or set a goal for yourself in the first place. Do those reasons still inspire you and fire up your fight instinct? Think of all the work you've put in to get to this point. You're right on the cusp of it all paying off!

- One very common stress during the taper is performance anxiety. I understand it. If you've worked your guts out for something, then you want to deliver when it matters. Otherwise, what is the point of all the preparation? It's here where mentality really separates the best from the rest. My advice to you, if you are feeling anxious in the run-up to whatever challenge you've set yourself, ask yourself if you have put everything you can into your preparation? If the answer is yes, then you've nothing to worry about. What more can you do? You've put absolutely everything you could into your preparation, so why worry? Instead, flip your anxiety on its head and focus on the preparation you have done. You should take confidence from the amount of work you've put in and start to visualize your success.

- It's okay every now and again to take a deep breath and acknowledge that you're on the cusp of the final test, and that the final test matters. Don't hide from that fact. You've taken on a challenge because you want to overcome it. The stakes are real but be confident in the body of work you've put together up to this point. Come D-Day you'll be ready to bang, and you'll be ready to back up your bull. During this purgatory period, instead of burning your energy with anxiety, build up your confidence and get ready to deliver.

- Visualization can help you tap into a very powerful and positive energy that will drive you towards your goal. More than that, it will build your confidence and self-belief as you stand at the foot of the mountain you are about to climb. Visualization helps you to prepare by anticipating what is to come. You can apply that to anything from a triathlon to a job interview. Anticipate the scenario and visualize your response to it.

- I want you to think about your own mountain and the challenge looming. What does the dark place look like for you? How deep will you have to dig, in order to prevail? One of the things I use to drive me into and through the dark place of pain is the fear of losing. I am ultra-competitive and the fear of losing galvanizes me through the hardest times. I urge you to connect with your fear of losing. It will drive you harder and further than you ever thought you could go. It will inspire you in the moments that you feel like quitting.

The Mountain

I was on the home straight and Thor waited at the finish line. I never thought I'd get the opportunity to get in the ring with him and do business. I never thought he had the stones for it. Now we were only hours away from settling this beef once and for all. I spent my last few days before the fight reflecting on a lot of things. I thought about things like time and opportunity, the ultra-fine margins between winning and losing, as well as the ruthless edge required to succeed.

In Chapter 5, you might remember I discussed failure and how I think about using it as a signpost directing me towards success. A sports psychologist told me to view failure as part of the journey rather than the destination.

The psychologist asked me the question, 'What if I told you that you had to suffer ten failures before you won World's Strongest Man?' That question helped me completely reconceive and reframe what failure is. Until then, failure had been a right ego bruiser. It was something to move on from as quickly as possible. I got too caught up in the emotion of the loss to grasp that failure also presented an opportunity to learn something. Once I began to take a second look at my failures, I realized I had loads to learn from them. It has been an incredible tool for me. I used it all the time on my journey from an absolute novice boxer to fighting Thor with millions of people watching from around the world.

This way of thinking is such a powerful tool. Obviously, it's helped me to learn, but it's also been a tool to rebuild my belief and self-confidence when I've had a knock. It's something hopeful in that respect. It made me think if I could learn from my failures, then I can avoid them second time around. As the final test loomed into view, I shifted my thinking from failures to opportunity. I flipped the way of thinking on its head – rather than counting down my failures, I counted up my opportunities.

How many more opportunities would I have got to win World's Strongest Man if I had not done it in 2017? There's no doubt that my obsession with bringing home the trophy meant that quitting without winning it was never an option. I always said I would win World's Strongest or die trying. But maybe I would have died trying. Would my body have held up for another attempt or would it have failed me? Would I have been able to mount another attempt if Alex had left me? Thankfully these questions don't have to be answered.

I did think about these things in the run-up to World's Strongest Man 2017. Failure was in the past, a stepping stone on the way to success. In front of me was the future, with the opportunity to implement what I'd learned from my failures and the chance to achieve my goals. Without doubt, the shift in mindset – from past failures to future opportunities – gave me a different type of motivation in those crucial couple of days before it. It focused me and it brought out a steely determination to maximize every single moment of the competition. In other words, I seized the day, every single day.

You don't have to tell someone from Stoke that

opportunities are rare. I had to put in massive amounts of hard work, as well as no end of sacrifice coupled with huge self-belief, to even get myself into a position where I had opportunities in the strongman world. Even when I broke into the elite class of strongmen, it required me to step up another level again in order to convert my opportunities into victories. I lived like a monk for two years in order to create the opportunity to win World's Strongest Man.

I knew I had limited opportunities in front of me with the fight. It was the first time two behemoths had stepped into the ring together – our combined weight was over 50 stone and we were confined inside a 24sq ft ring. The easy thing for a lot of people was to simply write off the fight as a stunt. But if you know me, you'd know I wouldn't have given two years of my life for a stunt. I wanted to win, and I wanted to win impressively. I wanted to show everybody the boxer that I had become. I drew on experience from my past to sharpen my focus, drill into my mindset, be absolutely ruthless and put in a clinical performance against Thor.

I called on the emotion I'd experienced when I'd failed. Without a doubt, the biggest hurt I've encountered in my professional career is losing. For someone like me, somebody who is, I'm going to say, *quite* competitive, it's hard to put into words what it feels like. The closest feeling I can compare it to, is death. I know that sounds extreme, but emotionally that is what losing feels like to me. It's death. Losing kills my hopes and dreams. Losing punctures whatever preconceptions I had of myself as an alpha, of being on top of the food chain. Losing demolishes my self-esteem. That's what losing has always felt like to me, the death of the person I thought I was. I appreciate this sounds a bit much, but how would you feel if you'd given everything to something and come up short?

Thankfully, after a couple of days I tend to get some perspective and I am able to reframe coming up short as one of those failures we've already talked about: a necessary stepping stone on the road to success. I pick myself back up and I'm ready to go again.

I tweaked my mentality a little bit due to the nature of boxing versus that of Strongman. It was one thing to try to outlift each other as Thor and I have done for years. It was quite another to climb into the ring to face off against each other in a fight. He was intent on inflicting major hurt on me. It was the first time I had encountered that level of sustained savagery coming my way since I was a doorman in Stoke.

Lindon helped me fine-tune this instinct. He's been around boxing for forty years and he knows what is asked of a man when he enters the ring. Boxing's demands are pretty stark. There couldn't be any doubts in my mind, or any hesitations in my actions once I crossed that threshold and the bell rang. I tapped into thinking that it is very primal – fight instinct – because in the ring it came down to Thor or me.

Lindon Newbon

The thing about Eddie is he's tenacious. I've seen people come into the gym, other big men over the years, and they look great on the bags, they look great on the pads and things like that. The first time they get hit, they don't like it. You hit Eddie Hall and he's going to hit you twice. It's as simple as that, that's just who he is. He's tenacious, which is great.

There's nothing quite like getting into the ring and fighting another man. If you've never sparred before, I urge you to go and do it. Obviously get your training in first under the supervision of a proper boxing coach. Don't be an idiot and hop into a sparring session with zero skills. You'll get found out very quickly. But once you've done your training and the coaches think you're ready, I urge you to hop into the ring. There is no buzz out there like it. It's just you and your opponent, and everything else fades away. You are entirely in the moment and consumed by it. In a weird way, it's peaceful. Or it would be if your opponent wasn't trying to punch you in the face.

The ring walk for the fight was unbelievable. The atmosphere was crackling. Even thinking about it now makes the hairs on my arms stand up. It was awesome in every sense.

You might recall in Chapter 7, The Smelling Salts, I discussed flow state. It's a period of performance in competition which is both instinctive and exceptional – everything seems to bend to your will, and you perform to the very best of your ability. Flow state is a tricky one. It's not like I have a switch I can flick to turn it on and off, but obviously I want to deliver my very best performance in anything I do. The seeds for a flow state performance are sown in the preparation.

As I've said, there's a big difference between *thinking* you're better than everybody else and *knowing* you're better than everybody else. I certainly learned that lesson in Strongman and there wasn't a single bit of complacency in my mindset before the fight. I prepared like I was facing the ultimate boss, even if it was only Thor. He's an athlete and I knew he was putting in work too.

Better every day – that's been my motto over the long period of sacrifice and suffering. That's what I've told myself when I've been working hard building my house of gains. However, in the last few hours before the final test, my mindset shifted from better every day, to be the best *today*. That's what it was about on fight night. Being at my very best.

Ultimately Thor came out with the victory on points, and I congratulated him as a professional. I lost the fight overall and make no excuses for that. I had my opportunities to put him down on the canvas and I took them. I give credit to Thor for getting back up and taking his chances as well.

I think the key thing to take away from this round is the importance of taking your opportunity when it comes. One thing I used to hone my ruthlessness was reflecting on certain regrets and I promised myself that I'd never feel that way again. I spoke with Ross Edgley about this very thing. Ross said, 'After I failed to complete a swim between Martinique and St. Lucia in the Caribbean, I remember going back to the hotel and I just remember feeling physically sick, just going, I never want to feel like this again, ever.'

I never want to feel like this again, ever. That's exactly the kind of regret I'm talking about. The kind of regret that makes you physically sick and you vow to yourself that there'll be no repeat. Use that to power you to your goal.

I asked James Haskell if he had any regrets looking back on his career. James told me, 'I've got probably two regrets. Not backing myself as much as I should have done. Also not celebrating the little victories, not celebrating those big moments, not celebrating those wins away because I was too focused on the next job.'

I think James makes a really good point about taking

some time with yourself to reflect on what you've achieved. In the aftermath of achievement it's about soaking up the victory and telling yourself, 'You did well today.'

Key Learnings

- The fight or flight instinct is a powerful force to try and harness. I want you to think about how you can find your own trigger to fight or flight. What aspects of your life are you unhappy with? How are you going to change the things in your life that you're not happy about? What is your pathway? Be under no illusion, you are in a fight. You are fighting for a better, more fulfilling life for yourself. It's why you need the primal energy coursing through your veins to get you through the struggle. It is *you* who decides what you're going to do and how you're going to do it. I'd put it to you that no matter what you're facing, it boils down to one question – are you going to fight or are you going to walk away?

- Victory or defeat begins with preparation. If there is a goal you want to achieve or a challenge you want to take on, the very best thing you can do to ensure success is to formulate a plan. Plans give you structure, they hold you accountable and they give you purpose. Build your house of gains. Make all of the hard work pay off in the most efficient way possible. Create an environment where you hold yourself accountable to your goals. Commit with all of your heart to whatever it is you want to achieve. Confidence in yourself and belief that you can achieve your goals are key. The person who wins is the person who believes they can!

- Who is the mentor figure in your challenge or goal? Nobody can do everything by themselves. It can be intimidating to reach out to someone who is an expert when you feel like a novice. Do it. It'll be the best decision you ever make. Who or what is your nemesis? Overcoming a nemesis requires a combination of hard work, sacrifice, dedication, consistency and self-belief. But the only real question is, how bad do you want it? Who are the people in your life who challenge you? Who are the people who pick you up when times are tough and celebrate your successes when they come along? These people are the allies in your life, the ones who support you in your journey towards your goal.

- Think about what motivates you and why you do the things you do. Embrace accountability. Saying your goal out loud to other people might make you feel uncomfortable. Nobody likes stepping out of their comfort zone but it's a necessary part of the journey too. Have you encountered moments of wanting to quit? I have used my relationship with people closest to me as motivation in the hardest times. Whatever journey you're on or challenge you're facing or goal you want to achieve, you'll find a deep well of motivation in making the people you love proud.

- I want you to think about the failures you've encountered in your life. How can you reframe your most recent failure as a positive which you can learn from? How can you use what you've learned to help you ultimately achieve your goal? Whatever you are trying to achieve, whatever goal you've set yourself, never lose sight of it. So much of life is failure. The most important part is to not let failure have the final word. Try, try and try again. It is the only way to succeed.

- The dark place exists in your mind. It is a reaction to pain. The question the pain is asking your mind is, are you going to quit or are you going to push through? The dark place is a gift because it confronts you with an extreme test of your abilities and it teaches you so much about yourself. Whatever it uncovers in you, will surprise you. My hope is that when you find yourself there, you will discover that you are stronger, more resilient and tougher than you thought you were.

- Measure your progress against your goals. There is nothing like a hard dose of reality to evaporate any complacent thoughts or behaviours. Always look at the goals you've set yourself and compare them with your progress to date. In sport, in business, in life, people are always searching for an edge. If you want to stay relevant, if you want to stay in contention for the medals, then you have to keep improving, innovating and pushing the boundaries. There's a big difference between *thinking* you're better than everybody else and *knowing* you're better than everybody else. View every opponent as the supreme threat; prepare and perform according to that belief. The things done every day lead to great achievements over time.

- Performance anxiety. I understand it. If you've worked your guts out for something, then you want to deliver when it matters. Flip your anxiety on its head and focus on the preparation you have done. You should take confidence from the amount of work you've put in and start to visualize your success. Visualization can help you tap into a very powerful and positive energy that will drive you towards your goal. Visualization helps you to prepare by anticipating what is to come. Anticipate the scenario and visualize your response to it.

- Be ruthless. Take your opportunities when they present themselves.

CONCLUSION

Backing Up Your Bull for Life

For a kid from Stoke who never wanted to be normal, I think I've done a pretty good job delivering that. There's nothing about my life that could ever be described as normal. I've added Dubai prize fighter to a CV that already includes world record holder, World's Strongest Man winner, social media star, TV presenter, doorman, truck mechanic. I've definitely not lived a normal life up to now and I don't plan on changing that any time soon.

I got what I needed out of the fight with Thor. A nice pot of cash to take care of my son Max and daughter Layla, as well as myself and Alex. That's the thing isn't it? At the top of the mountain . . . is another mountain to climb. In my life, I need mountains to climb. The mountains fill the void for me. They lighten the lonely, empty feeling that comes with depression.

So, what will be the next challenge? I'm looking at what options are on the table. The fight has opened up some more avenues and I'll see what opportunities I want to explore. As you know, Arnold Schwarzenegger has been my hero ever since he rocked up to a biker bar in *Terminator 2: Judgment Day* and the film business is something that really interests me. I'd love to be rubbing shoulders with the people I admire in that world, and that's something I'm pursuing.

Arnold changed my life. I can say honestly, if it wasn't for Arnold Schwarzenegger, I would never have got into bodybuilding and I'd never have become World's Strongest Man. He inspired me to get up off my backside and go down to the gym when I was depressed.

I hope I can be an inspiration to you, too, and to anyone who is struggling or suffering out there. I hope that my story can show you that nothing is impossible, whatever your dreams are, whatever obstacles that are in front of you, whatever situation you find yourself in – nothing is impossible.

What do you want to do with your life? What do you want from it? Do you want to be a sheep like I was? I can't answer for you what burns in your heart's desire, but I've shared with you the mental tools I've used to achieve my dreams. You have access to the same tools, and you can use them to achieve your dreams.

Whatever the challenge, whatever the obstacle in front of you, there are tools you can use to overcome them. The very first obstacle you'll encounter is yourself in the form of the fight or flight instinct. You will find a million reasons why you can't, couldn't or won't do something, and at the root of every single one of those reasons is the flight instinct. You're scared. You need to take control of that instinct and turn it upside down. You take every single one of those reasons why you can't and turn them on their head – make them the reasons why you must do it. Instead of 'I can't become World's Strongest Man because I'm a mechanic' it becomes 'I must become World's Strongest Man because I'm a mechanic.' Use the things that you allowed to hold you back as fuel to power you forward. In that way you'll unlock your superpower – the fight instinct.

The fight instinct is primal energy and it's powerful. It's

an adrenaline surge that gives your physical power a turbo boost, as well as fortifying your mindset. It puts you in a zone where physically and mentally you believe you are unbeatable. I found a way to activate that power at will. The things in my life that I wanted to change, the things that made me unhappy, became a way to trigger the fight instinct and all the power that came with it. It gave me an intensity and determination to change my life, with Strongman being the way to do it. What are the things in your life that you want to change? What are the things that make you unhappy? Harness them to activate your fight instinct. Channel the power it unleashes into something that you believe will change your life. There will be times when you feel like you can't change things no matter how much time and energy you invest. In those moments, my advice to you is to remember that you have no control over the past or indeed the future, but you have absolute control over the here and now. What are you going to do with it?

Everyone needs a vision for their life. What is yours? Visualization is a major tool in my locker, one I use again and again. Whatever the dream is for you, whatever the goal you want to achieve, close your eyes and see it happening. See in your mind what it means for you and how it would change your life. Let it become a symbol in your mind that you can draw on to drive you forward in the hard times.

Once you know what it is you want to achieve, that's more than half the battle. With your goal in mind, now is the time to plan and prepare. I've always loved the saying 'Fail to prepare, prepare to fail'. With the best will in the world, it's not enough to say you want to do something, you have to put in place a plan that is realistic and achievable. You have to craft a plan that is going to give you a structure, with clear, measurable stepping stones to your goal. It is critical to success. At this point you need to think about every angle and aspect of what you want to achieve. Take the time to map the journey ahead and formulate a strategy which gives you the best chance of succeeding. Once you have a plan, commit it to paper. Know what exactly you're doing at every step along the way.

Writing it down makes you accountable to your plan. If you miss a session, it's on you. You have to live with the gnawing guilt of sacking it off. More than that, it opens the door to doubt. There is a reason a session is in the plan and if you miss it then you're deviating from the path towards your goal. With your plan you are creating an environment where you have zero excuses and full accountability.

I want you to think about how you can break down your plan into smaller elements. For the fight with Thor, I broke my plan down into smaller elements like boxing skills, fitness, diet and recovery. Think about the elements you can break your plan down into. How can those elements work together in the most efficient way? Each element is a brick and putting those bricks together builds you a house of gains.

Formulating a plan should make you excited, and maybe even a little bit daunted by the prospect of what you're trying to do. If it doesn't get the heart beating and the juices flowing, it's time to think again. You really need to be in love with the process that underpins what you're trying to achieve. Anything worth doing is going to involve struggle and setbacks. When you encounter them, you're going to double down and work harder. My advice to you is to make the hard work as easy as possible. Think about how you can build your life around whatever it is you're trying to achieve. It's a big commitment but it's one worth doing if you're serious about what you're aiming to do.

If you are serious, really serious about what you want to achieve, then you have to find yourself a mentor. I promise you, mentors are all around you. *Terminator 2* is on the TV every other week, after all. Think of who your first hero was. What qualities did they have that made them your hero? You're a smart cookie, you can look at them and how they acted and figure out how you can incorporate their values and behaviour into your life. I'll be your mentor if you want. I'm sharing with you my mindset and all of the things I've used to achieve what I've achieved. I want to inspire and aid you whatever way I can. I might not be there spotting you in the gym, but you can probably *visualize* pretty easily what I would be saying to you as you squeeze out those last few reps.

What I'm saying to you is, there are mentors everywhere around you if you know how to look. The role models and the heroes are one type of mentor, but you'll also find there are mentors in your life that are just waiting to be asked about advice or for help. They are only too eager to share their knowledge and their insight. Don't be scared or intimidated; mentors love nothing more than helping someone who is eager to learn. Think about the kind of mentor you want to help you on your journey. It might be a teacher who can help you get the exam results you want or a running coach who can help you achieve a better race time.

We all have allies in our life who challenge us to be better, tell us the truth and don't blow smoke up our backsides. These are the people who have your back and you have theirs. These allies support you in your drive towards your goal, they pick you up in the bad times and celebrate with you in the good. Think about the people in your life who are your allies. How can they support you in your quest? And how can you support them in their quest?

Every challenge has a nemesis. For me it was Thor, but for you it could be a time or score you want to beat, or perhaps it might well be another opponent who rubs you up the wrong way. There is no doubt there is a tinge of darkness driving your motivation when you encounter a nemesis. It comes from a place of hurt and hate, I think. It will help drive you past your own limitations. The word quit will never even enter your mind when you're facing a nemesis. It is something you can harness and channel into your own performance.

I had Thor and my hate for him was the darkness which drove me. I also have a lot of light in my life too. I have my wife and kids as well as my parents and brothers and of course my dear departed nan. Making them proud gives me a very deep sense of motivation, and the will to push through the painful moments. Who are the people you want to make proud? How can you use those relationships to give you a deep well of motivation to draw on during testing times?

You're going to encounter periods when you want to quit and walk away from what you're doing. One of the tools in my locker that I use and have found so powerful for me is being outspoken about my goals and the things I want to achieve. I use it to put pressure on myself to back up my bull. In the same way I believe you can use the same tool to stop you from quitting. Tell the people who you want to make proud what you want to do with your life. They love you and they will support you. You don't want to be seen as flaky or not able to follow through. By sharing your goal with the people who you want to make proud, it erects a barrier between you and quitting. You might not like stepping out of your comfort zone but it's pretty much undeniable that it'll make you work harder to try and achieve what you said you'll do.

I've spoken to you about the special people in my life, especially my relationship with my wife Alex and my nan. I want you to think about the people in your life who love and support you. Love is an emotion that you can harness to power you through pretty much anything in life. You earn your happiness in this life through suffering. Anything worth doing requires hard work and, inevitably, hard work comes with a degree of suffering. None of us enjoy suffering, and yet it is through suffering that you grow. It is through suffering that you take those vital steps towards your goal or your dream. It is through suffering that you attain true happiness.

Who do you fight for? Who do you want to make proud? Who do you feel you have an obligation to deliver for? Who ignites your motivation when you need it?

We all have someone we love who we want to fight for and make proud.

In choosing to take on a challenge or to try to achieve a goal, you have agreed to undertake a journey. You have a destination in your mind which you've visualized and you are intent on getting there. Inevitably, you will encounter many setbacks and failures on your journey. The key is to not allow those setbacks and failures to dishearten you. I ask you what is your reaction to failure? Does it inspire you to commit to work harder or does it discourage you? It's perfectly natural to feel disappointed and demoralized in the aftermath of failure. It's an ego-bruising experience that will put you in a very dark hole if you let it.

You need to reframe failure and setbacks as necessary parts of your journey towards your ultimate goal, whatever that might be. It's easy to get lost in the pain of failure or in the frustration of a setback. But you have to ask yourself how is wallowing in those emotions helping you to achieve your goal? You need to divorce your ego and your emotions from the failure and instead learn from it. Why did you fail? What did the failure reveal about the elements you need to work on? How will you work on those elements?

It's important to keep in mind the big picture as well. I failed a hell of a lot along the way to my ultimate goal of winning World's Strongest Man. Keep your failures in perspective and use them to work for you. It's not to say that you will ever enjoy failure, but you can welcome the opportunity to learn. It's a waste of a failure if you don't take that experience and learn from it. Hopefully if you do that, you won't repeat the same mistakes again.

The final thing I'd say to you in relation to failure is there is absolutely zero shame in coming up short if you've given everything and more to a cause. If you pushed yourself further than you ever thought you could go, that is success in itself. Even if you don't achieve what you set out to achieve, think about where you started from and be proud of how much you've learned and grown along the way.

I believe we all have to suffer for our happiness and inevitably suffering leads to pain. Sometimes we have to endure a hell of a lot of pain for our happiness – the period I refer to as the dark place. I believe the dark place is a gift. It is a crucible of pain and suffering that will reveal your true nature. The dark place confronts you with an extreme test of your abilities and teaches you so much about yourself. Whatever it uncovers in you, will surprise you. My hope is that when you find yourself there, you will discover that you are stronger, more resilient and tougher than you ever thought you were.

The dark place is your mind's reaction to pain. The question the pain is asking is are you going to quit or are you going to push through? It's a question only you can answer. It will go a long way to determining if you succeed or fail in your ultimate goal.

To pass through the flame of pain, you need to be obsessed. Obsession has a dark underbelly. It can drive you to incredible achievement, but it can also goad you into taking risks with your physical and mental health. I've shared with you my own personal struggles with my mental health. The one thing I would beg of you: if anything that I've talked about strikes a chord, then please speak to someone. Talk to a friend or talk to your doctor. Talk to someone because there is no need for you to suffer in silence. There is no glory in trying to overcome depression by yourself. It's the darkest of dark places but there is always a way back to the light.

As you put in hard work and begin to improve, the big trap to avoid at this point is complacency. There are three types to watch out for – the smug git, the prisoner of success and the competitor complacency. The smug git is an obvious trap, but it doesn't stop the best of us from falling into it. It is human nature to derive satisfaction from improvement. The danger with falling into the trap of being a smug git is that you're so pleased with yourself and the work you've done so far, that it leaves you ignorant of the dangers you face and blind to your deficiencies. Without a doubt, this kind of complacency is the enemy of excellence.

There are a few tools you can use to guard against the smug git. Have an honesty session with yourself. Have you got room to improve or are you satisfied with where you're at? I'll give you a hint: the answer to this question is always no. You always have things you can work on and seek to improve! If you need some extra motivation, use the visualization tool to see yourself failing in the worst possible way. I guarantee you there is nothing quite like the fear of falling on your arse to get your motivation back sharpish.

The other great tool to use against the smug git is to compare your progress against your goals. There's nothing quite like the gap between where you think you are and where you actually are to kick your arse back into gear. You wrote down your goals, goals that are measurable and definitive. How close or how far are you from achieving those goals? You can duck or fudge the answer. You're either hitting your markers or you're not. If you've already blown past your goals, then reassess and aim higher!

Accountability is a terrific tool to keep you on track in this period where it is tempting to start cutting sessions short or skipping out on them all together. Like I said before, it's human nature to ease up, especially if you have been pushing yourself very hard to get better. Once you see some improvement, it's so easy to fall into thinking or acting like a smug git. It might be in the manner in which you prepare, the intensity of your training sessions, or your desire to improve. Having a structure around you to keep you accountable to your plan and committed to your sessions is another great tool to guard against complacency.

There is a type of complacency which is rooted in process – you can become a prisoner to your own success.

It's all too easy to become married to a set routine that has yielded results. But in order to get better you have to be constantly evolving your approach. You have to be curious about what you could change to your way of doing things, then you have to be brave and implement changes that you think might help you. You have to innovate and keep evolving, even in the face of a short-term dip in results.

Whatever opponent you face, as you prepare and improve, complacency can creep into your mindset and you can underestimate whoever or whatever it is you're up against. Correct this flaw in your thinking. Always prepare as though you are facing the ultimate boss. Think about the work you need to do to overcome and prevail. Never, ever think you've done enough to achieve your goal. As soon as you do that, you'll start slackening off. Stay working, stay hungry. You set the standards of excellence, not your opponent or anyone else. You set the bar on your performance and you should be aiming as high as possible. If you let other people dictate your standards to you, then you'll never achieve your potential.

All of these tools help to keep you on a consistent path towards your goal. Consistency is key. Improvement is the gift consistency confers on you if you have the grit to get through the grind every day. It allows you to develop routines and build momentum towards your goal. Consistency is the difference between failure and success. There is nothing magical or mysterious about what I am telling you. Remember, the things done every day lead to great achievements over time.

If you want to squeeze every last drop of potential out of yourself then it's worth remembering how the best of the best have done it before you. You have to love the process inherent in the challenge or goal you've set yourself. So much of what makes the very best, the very best is that they love the consistent hard work that they put in. They graft to get better. If you want to be like them, then you have to graft for it too. There are no shortcuts for you or work-arounds. You've got to work your backside off, day in, day out. Simple as.

A competitive nature definitely helps. Some of us are more competitive than others, but we all have a competitive streak. You might recall that I said I was very good at nurturing my nature. You can nurture your competitive streak and use it to get better. Remember the feeling of failure or loss and use it to fuel your appetite to improve and get better. Nobody enjoys losing. Take the pain and use it to drive an obsession to be excellent.

Failure, setbacks and losses are all part of the journey when you're striving to be the best. You need to embrace failure as a means to learn lessons. There's a reason you've failed. Find it and fix it. No matter the failure or the obstacle, you need to find a way to keep moving forward towards your goal. The thing you'll learn from all of the experiences of failure is resilience and perseverance are what define you, not failure.

What makes you resilient? You have to be willing to suffer for your happiness. You have to view failure and adversity as an opportunity to grow. More than that I think you have to enjoy being constantly pushed to your limits and beyond. You have to enjoy the discomfort that comes with always being challenged every day.

You have to bring a forensic eye to your own preparation and development. Think about all of the elements that go into your routine. Remember you're trying to build a house of gains from those elements. Be brave – if something isn't working then change it. Stay focused on yourself and what you're trying to achieve. Search for anything that can give you an edge and use it.

At some point you're going to encounter the haters, the people who say you can't do something. Don't give them a second thought. Keep a laser-like focus on yourself and what you are trying to achieve. Set your own standards and strive to get better every day. Through hard work and consistency, you can blow past what you and anyone else around you thought you were capable of. You must take responsibility for your own development and empower yourself to do the things you need to do in order to get better.

You are responsible for your mindset. Be under no illusions, mindset is the difference; it is the thing that separates you from everybody else. You need to remember this especially as you transition into the final period, when the mountain you've set yourself to climb looms into view. This is a golden opportunity to resolve any mental doubts or performance anxiety that might be lingering in your mind. Use the time as an opportunity to pull out your mental tools, examine them and make sure that everything is in good working order. It'll give you tremendous comfort and confidence to know that you have no lingering doubts, that your mindset is on point and that you're ready to go.

Reflect on your journey to this point. Think about the reasons you took on a challenge or set a goal for yourself in the first place. Do those reasons still inspire you and fire up your fight instinct? Think of all the work you've put in to get to this point. You're right on the cusp of cashing it in. Given how much time, energy and effort you've expended to get to this point, it's natural for a little bit of performance anxiety to creep in. You want to deliver a performance when it matters, and you're concerned you won't be able to do it.

Ask yourself if you have put everything you can into your preparation? If the answer is yes, then you've nothing to worry about. What more can you do? You've put absolutely everything you could into your preparation, so why worry? Flip your anxiety on its head and focus on the preparation you have done. Take confidence from the amount of work you've put in and use this time instead to visualize your success.

You're on the cusp of the final test, and the final test matters to you. Don't hide from that fact. You've taken on a challenge because you want to overcome it. You should take stock of your journey and take confidence from the work that you've put in to get yourself to this point. Come D-Day you'll be ready to bang, and you'll be ready to back up your bull.

I want you to think about the opportunities you will get in your life to achieve your goal or conquer your dream. Opportunities are rare. You need to be ruthless when they present themselves. Remember the work you've put in to get to this point, remember the pain you've suffered through. Seize the moment, and it might just be a split-second moment, but when it presents itself, be ruthless and take it.

Epilogue

So, as you probably knew all along, I got in the ring and I gave it a good go, against one of the biggest men on the planet. He hit the canvas. I hit the canvas. But ultimately, I lost on points. Fair play to Thor. He must have worked very hard. He looked good in the ring. His fitness and conditioning were good. And I feel like he fought more tactically than I did. Now, it's time to reflect. It's time to think about what I achieved, what didn't go my way, and what I learned.

On the achievement side, I think it's obvious – I went from knowing nothing about boxing to stepping in the ring for a fight watched by *more than 30 million people* around the world. I hope those people watching had a good time. I've got to say, I did. It was a complete blast. It was incredible to get in the ring and throw bombs at each other for twenty-four minutes. I can hand on heart say I have never had such a thrill in all my life. I absolutely loved it. And think Thor and I pulled off something pretty special.

The other thing that I can take away from this fight, as you've heard throughout this book, is every time I was dealt a bad hand – Covid, tearing my bicep – it didn't stop me. Even in the fight itself, I'm proud that I took a punch from a fellow strongman like Thor. Get in a boxing ring and you're risking your life – that is the top and bottom of it – especially bearing in mind the power that we both had on display. We knew the potential consequences, but we still had the balls to get in the ring and do it. I'm proud that when Thor landed me on my back, I got back up on my own two feet and swung back at him. If you watch the fight, even in the last moments, I'm trying to land a big right. I never gave up; I fought right to the bell. I did well. But, at the end of the day, not well enough. I got into that arena and I fought as hard as I could. But it wasn't enough on the night.

With that in mind, I'd be lying if I said I thought that was the best boxing that I could have done on the night, and I feel a little bit like I let Lindon down there. We worked for a long time on getting my boxing skills to the highest level, and, in the heat of the fight, I let my emotions get the better of me. That's a bit of a shame, I think. Because it's two years of my life that I've put into this boxing game. Two years for one fight. In the days afterwards, I felt a bit deflated, if I'm being honest. It had been a long, hard, vigorous, mentally draining, physically draining journey. And then, all of a sudden, it's done. Well, look – I've been here before. I've had competitions where I came third. You do all that training, all that prep, all that money, all that mindset, all that energy – everything put into one thing. And then you come third, and for a day or two, you're like, 'Why did I bother? All that for *this*?' And I admit that I experienced a little bit of that this time; putting in all that hard work and not getting the win, it's natural to ask yourself what it was all for. Being the person that I am, that competitive monster inside me, it's quite a hard thing to take and move on from. But I'll also say this: losing *any* competition is tough. But you have got to learn to take it and accept it. Not everything is going to go your way all the time. And this fight didn't go my way. Losing and failing is a big part of success. So, like I've done before, I get up, I dust myself off and I get on with it. That's what I call a champion's mindset. Win or lose, you can always act like a champion.

I'll tell you what, I've learned a hell of a lot. I've learned a lot of skills as an athlete, as a boxer, but I've also learned a lot about myself. One of the real lessons here is about humility. In the lead-up to the fight, I went wild. I went absolutely wild, and I thought, I really hate this guy. I used that as an excuse to play mind games and do and say things I wouldn't normally do. There are some things that I regret, things I wish I hadn't done. I've only ever watched the big hype fights, the Tyson Furys and the Muhammad Alis and the Conor McGregor fights where there's a lot of talk and a lot of theatre. And in hindsight, I went too far. In reality, as much as I hated the guy, I think I should have been a bit more composed. I think if I had, I would have shown more respect for the sport. And a bit more respect to Thor.

And on that, it's a good moment to say well done Thor

for the fight. Seeing it now, I can appreciate Thor for who he is, for the things he's achieved in his life, and for all the graft that he put into this fight. Thor's a giant in the strongman world. There are plenty of giants in strongman – and I believe the world needs people like us. I've never wanted to be an ordinary bloke, just doing my own thing. I've always wanted to do something special, to be different. I can see that quality in him too. As for the rivalry and bitterness between us, I think it's time for Thor and me to move on. I feel like I have achieved some closure. I don't want all the successes in my career, and all the adventures I'm going to go on, to be overshadowed by something he said to me back in 2017. I've had my scrap now, I punched Thor in the face, and I'm over it. In fact, I have to say I'm thankful to Thor. Like I said earlier in this book, having a worthy opponent can bring out the best in you. And I think that's what happened here.

Right now, I can see that I have a huge amount to be thankful for. I'm grateful for the people around me. I have a fantastic support system. This isn't an easy moment in my career. There was this massive, public, worldwide lead-up. And I suppose everyone has their own perception of who's going to do what and what's going to happen. As a result, some of the backlash online has been pretty rough. I can laugh it off, but even so, I'm grateful for the people around me right now holding me together and keeping me going. Most of all my family. They've been great at helping me remember what's important. And what's important to me is *them*. That's the most important thing in my life: my wife and kids.

Right at the start of this book we talked about fight or flight. I didn't run away from any challenge that this fight posed for me. I stood up and I took the blows – physical, mental, Covid, whatever – I took them all on the chin. It wasn't enough on the night, but as I've said, failure is just a stepping stone on the road to success. Like the psychologist once said to me, 'What if you had to lose ten times to win World's Strongest Man?' I know that, in the long term, losing to Thor is going to lead me to bigger and better success in the future. I felt the need to prove something to the world with this fight. But the most important thing is the people who you don't need to prove anything to – your family. Whatever my next adventure is, wherever this takes me next, I'm going to be doing it side by side with them. Because it doesn't matter how hard things get in life, you should never give up. You should always take losses and failures and defeat as little detours along the way. It's got to happen. And it's important to say that you don't get to the top without a setback. But you also don't get to the top if, when you experience a setback, you do nothing with it, or you dig yourself into a hole of negativity. I see this loss as an opportunity. It's an opportunity to better myself. To go forward in my life, to keep doing amazing things, to keep staying positive and to keep supporting the people that I love.

On that hot and humid night in March 2022, I got in the ring and rumbled with Thor and made history. Now the new Titan Weight category of boxing, and championship belt, for the really big men, the strongmen, the wrestlers, the giants of sport, has been established. We've created something that people really want to see, and I want to be a part of it. I'm going to keep on fighting. All I see ahead is a world of opportunity, the chance to meet incredible people, to work on fantastic projects and keep doing everything I know and love. And I wouldn't be anything without the people I love. With my family on my side, and with you on my side, I will always be a winner.

Guys, I hope you've enjoyed this book as much as I've enjoyed writing it. I hope you've learned something, like I have. And I hope it inspires you to go on your own adventures.

Keep being awesome and enjoy life. Stay strong. Stay positive. And most of all, never, *ever*, give up.

Big love,

The Beast.

Acknowledgements

There are a number of people I want to acknowledge for their contribution in putting this book together. Firstly, I want to thank my incredible wife, Alex. I am where I am today because of all your incredible love and support. I want to thank my mum and dad, Helen and Stephen. I hope I make you proud every single day. To my kids, Layla and Max, you bring so much light and joy into my life. Everything I do, I do for you both.

Shout out to my boxing trainer Lindon Newbon. It's been a hell of a journey together and I've learned so much from you. Thank you for agreeing to work with me and for giving so much of yourself to the quest. I also have to say a thank you to my best mate and training partner, Patrick Gale. From morning walks to leg days in the gym to sparring in the ring you've been there every step of the way. Thanks to Josh Middleton for all his hard work in the ring to help me prepare for the fight. Thanks to Aaron Sharpe for his help too.

I'd like to thank all the team at W.F. Howes who first published the audiobook. Dominic White, thank you for all your support and encouragement. Lewis Hampson, thank you for your guidance and patience during our recording sessions. Laura Smith, thank you for your tremendous work in trawling through the archive to find just the right clip to use. Thanks to Jack Ramm and Thomas Aspell for their help in gathering my thoughts and piecing together the story of my boxing journey. Thanks to James Haskell, Paddy McGuinness and Ross Edgley for being so generous with their time and for sharing their insightful stories with me. Thanks to Ed Faulkner and the whole team at Allen & Unwin and Atlantic Books for publishing the book edition.

Finally, thanks to all my fans for their support, for liking and subscribing to my YouTube channel. This book is for all of you.

Big love,

The Beast.